M000023586

Presented To:

From:

Date:

THE REALITY OF **ANGELIC MINISTRY** TODAY

BOOK TWO

DANCING WITH
ANGELS 2

THE REALITY OF **ANGELIC MINISTRY** TODAY

BOOK TWO

DANCING WITH ANGELS 2

*The Role of the Holy Spirit and Open Heavens
in Activating Your Angelic Visitations*

KEVIN BASCONI

© Copyright 2011—Kevin Basconi

All rights reserved. This book is protected by the copyright laws of the United States of America. This book may not be copied or reprinted for commercial gain or profit. The use of short quotations or occasional page copying for personal or group study is permitted and encouraged. Permission will be granted upon request. Unless otherwise identified, Scripture quotations are taken from the New King James Version. Copyright © 1982 by Thomas Nelson, Inc. Used by permission. All rights reserved. Scripture quotations marked WNT are taken from the 1902 Weymouth New Testament by Richard Francis Weymouth. Not copyrighted in the United States of America. All emphasis within Scripture quotations is the author's own. Please note that Destiny Image's publishing style capitalizes certain pronouns in Scripture that refer to the Father, Son, and Holy Spirit, and may differ from some publishers' styles. Take note that the name satan and related names are not capitalized. We choose not to acknowledge him, even to the point of violating grammatical rules.

DESTINY IMAGE® PUBLISHERS, INC.

P.O. Box 310, Shippensburg, PA 17257-0310

"Speaking to the Purposes of God for This Generation and for the Generations to Come."

This book and all other Destiny Image, Revival Press, MercyPlace, Fresh Bread, Destiny Image Fiction, and Treasure House books are available at Christian bookstores and distributors worldwide.

For a U.S. bookstore nearest you, call 1-800-722-6774.
For more information on foreign distributors, call 717-532-3040.
Reach us on the Internet: www.destinyimage.com.

ISBN 13 TP: 978-0-7684-3821-5
ISBN 13 Ebook: 978-0-7684-8982-8

For Worldwide Distribution, Printed in the U.S.A.

1 2 3 4 5 6 7 8 9 10 11 / 13 12 11

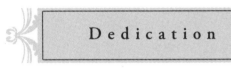

Dedication

This book

is

dedicated

to

God the Father, God the Son, and God the Holy Spirit.

Without

You Guys,

of this

would

have

been

possible!

Acknowledgments

I want to thank my precious wife, Kathy Basconi, for her love, patience, long hours of proofreading, and help with the entire process of writing these books.

I love you!

Truth revealed! Kevin has the ability to fuse spiritual revelation with practical relevance. This book is a must-read for every person who wants to move forward and understand the supernatural realm of Christ's angelic hosts and how God desires to have them work in our life every day. *Dancing with Angels 2* is sound biblical teaching that will give you the proper keys that will help you to activate and release God's angels to work on your behalf!

BRIAN LAKE
Brian Lake Ministries
Keepers of the Flame International Church

Kevin has fast become an authority on the ministry of angels today. His fresh, biblical insights will captivate you as you read this timely and inspiring book. The stories of his amazing experiences will leave you breathless, causing you to desire more of the supernatural realm of the Spirit. *Dancing With Angels 2* will challenge you to develop a deeper intimacy with God, resulting in your own angelic visitations.

GARY OATES
Author, *Open My Eyes, Lord*

If you are like me and wonder how God's angels are working in your life, then Kevin Basconi's book *Dancing With Angels 2:*

The Role of the Holy Spirit and Open Heavens in Activating Your Angelic Visitations is a must-read. This book will encourage and inspire you. Kevin deflates the mystical mindset of many believers that Kingdom encounters are for the very few, the so-called "elite" believers. Kevin gives easy steps and practical scriptural advice that can help any believer to access the Kingdom of Heaven and the realm of God's angels. This book will stir you to reach for the full potential God has for you. It's an essential book that is so necessary for every believer who is pressing into God and wants to go deeper with Him at this time. Every pastor, church leader, and believer would benefit from reading this extraordinary book!

Dr. Jonathan Tan
London, England

In *Dancing With Angels 2,* Kevin's second book of the trilogy *The Reality of Angelic Ministry Today,* he continues to build a biblical foundation for the role of angelic ministry and activity today. Kevin shares several simple ways that will help ordinary people recognize and cooperate with God's angels to accomplish the Lord's will on the earth. Throughout the book, Kevin shares powerful yet practical testimonies, both personal and from others, explaining how angels are active today and can become more active in our everyday lives as we learn to entertain them. He emphasizes how this is especially true when we are actively pursuing the Lord and seeking to obey Him in accomplishing His purposes. He also strongly reminds us from the Scriptures that *"we have not because we ask not"* in regard to our understanding and participation in angelic ministry.

One of the greatest strengths of the book is how Kevin shares his experiences in his quest to know the glory of God—or open heavens—which we are promised will become more and more revealed upon the earth through the Church as we draw nearer to the end of this age. His personal testimonies create a hunger in the reader to seek and know that glory for oneself.

The book ends with a solidly biblical account of the role of each believer as a royal priesthood in the order of Melchizedek and how we must view ourselves as God sees us—as priests and prophets who have been given authority on the earth. Kevin also emphasizes how personal holiness and spiritual character are required if we are to truly and fully see God's Kingdom and His glory known around us. However, he also reminds us that walking in holiness and obedience is a process which the Holy Spirit will guide us through.

Kevin has written a biblical account of how, as believers, we can live under and have access to the heavenly realms where Jesus lived as a Man yet also the Son of God.

Finally, both Kevin and Kathy remind us that we are living on the threshold of the revealing of God's judgments on the earth. However, they both encourage the readers to pray for mercy and be ready to be a vessel of honor in the greatest days to have been chosen to live upon the earth.

PASTOR DAVID WHITE
Pastor, Morningstar Fellowship
Wilkesboro, North Carolina

Kevin and Kathy Basconi are truly a couple who know their God. They have had numerous experiences in the glory realm of the Kingdom and have enormous, authentic insight to share with you, the reader. *Dancing With Angels 2,* the second book in the trilogy, will bless, encourage, and empower you.

PATRICIA KING
XPmedia.com

Contents

Foreword

It is my pleasure to write a brief foreword to *Dancing With Angels 2: The Role of the Holy Spirit and Open Heavens in Activating Your Angelic Visitations*. This is Kevin's second book about angelic ministry and the realms of God's angelic hosts. Kevin knows first-hand the truths he is communicating! Immediately upon hearing the title, I thought of this verse: *"I tell you the truth, you shall see heaven open, and the angels of God ascending and descending on the Son of Man"* (John 1:51 NIV). Jesus told his new disciple, Nathaniel, that he was going to see and experience open heavens, and there is no greater authority on this subject than Jesus! Open heavens were not just for biblical times; open heavens are for us today! Whether it was Jacob dreaming, Stephen prior to drawing his last breath, or John getting the Book of Revelation, the Bible is replete with examples of our elders in the faith who experienced the heavens being opened. Kevin, through real-life experiences, shows how you can experience open heavens in your own life.

Something will be birthed within you as you read this book; a hunger will be developed and a passion stirred to experience more of God in your life. As you will read the examples of open heavens and angelic visitations, you will not be content until you see the heavens opened over your life. This book makes that possibility seem quite easy and practical! Buckle your seat belts, and get ready to enjoy *Dancing With Angels 2*...your life and walk with God may never be the same!

PASTOR ALAN KOCH
Christ Triumphant Church
Lee's Summit, Missouri

DANCING WITH ANGELS 2

In the first book of this trilogy, *Dancing With Angels 1: How to Work With Angels in Your Life*, I shared numerous experiences I have lived through with God's angels. In that book, I sought to outline and equip people to have those same ongoing experiences as well. In this book, our goal is to expound upon those testimonies of angelic ministry in the lives of ordinary people by including dozens of additional testimonies of angelic visitations that we were not able to include in the first manuscript.

My prayer is that you would be entertained, enlightened, and empowered to activate these same kinds of life-changing angelic encounters in your life. As I have previously illustrated, my life was transformed when I began to "entertain" angels that were beginning to visit my space. This was the direct result of a vision of Christ I experienced as a new believer. In that initial vision, Jesus was surrounded by four angelic beings. During that vision, the Lord said to me, "Today I am appointing these angels to your ministry." This perplexed me, as I had no ministry. However, the Lord did indeed launch me into international ministry in short order. Those same four angels played a key role in that process. This activation was a direct result of angelic visitations and encounters I have previously outlined in the first book of this trilogy

I also sought to outline and establish several easy methods that would allow anyone to access the Kingdom of Heaven and the realms of angels. This is possible for you because of the God-ordained or *kairos* moment of time that we are currently living in. I want to stress that it is vital that we use sound principles and practices when seeking to entertain angels. The only *legal* avenue to access the angelic realm is through Jesus Christ and His atonement on the Cross of Calvary. I also established that the Lord Christ Jesus embraced and employed angelic ministry in His earthly life and ministry, and what's more, the Lord has every intention of continuing to utilize angelic ministry to impact the earth. Angels play a vital role in God's end-time plans for the earth and humankind. In this book, I will elaborate on my theories concerning Christ and the angelic ministry and intervention in His temporal or earthly life. We will also explore how Christ continues to employ angels today.

In the first book of this trilogy, I illustrated a powerful visitation of Jesus Christ that I experienced in April of 2007. Within that vision, the Lord gave me an important parabolic experience that occurred in the realms of Heaven, or the "heavenly places." A parabolic experience could be defined as an event that has an obvious meaning. However, they can also carry a deeper moral or spiritual lesson that you can learn from by studying it in more detail.

This passage exemplifies that powerful vision well:

[God] *raised us up together, and made us sit together in the heavenly places in Christ Jesus, that in the ages to come He might show the exceeding riches of His grace in His kindness toward us* [humanity] *in Christ Jesus* (Ephesians 2:6-7).

I believe that these kinds of visitations and supernatural experiences will begin to become more commonplace with ordinary folks who are truly seeking the Lord with all of their hearts. No longer will angelic visitations and visions be limited to "chosen vessels." The Lord will open up this realm and ordinary people's eyes as the gift of discerning of spirits is reestablished within the Body of Christ (see Deut. 4:29; Jer. 29:13).

In that vision, Jesus gave me revelations about a coming move of God, or what I termed "global healing revivals and outpourings." I prophesied that ordinary folks were going to be used by the Lord to ignite these outpourings as they learned to co-labor with God's angels in a similar way that the Argentinean revival was sparked in 1949. My prayer is that this book would be a tool that the Lord would use to equip the Body of Christ to accomplish those same end-time mandates upon the earth.

In this book, *Dancing With Angels 2: The Role of the Holy Spirit and Open Heavens in Activating Your Angelic Visitations,* I will continue to build upon several scriptural principles associated with the angelic realm. I am going to examine in great detail the importance of the Holy Spirit and His role in implementing or *activating* angelic ministry. The Holy Spirit's ministry and role are extremely significant and of great consequence to our pursuit. I will seek to elaborate on the various ways you can work in symphony with the Holy Spirit in relationship to angelic ministry.

I will also have the opportunity to expand on several ideas and concepts that I was not able to elaborate upon fully because of the limitation of space in the first book. I pray these testimonies and scriptural principles will encourage you and build your faith to accomplish all that the Lord has called you to do at this crucial hour. We will investigate more of my theories about Christ Jesus' mindset in relation to angelic ministry in *Dancing With Angels 2*. We will examine several scriptural passages that illuminate Christ's ongoing interaction with angels. By elaborating upon these and other instances of angelic ministry found in the Bible, we can help to build upon the foundations laid in the first book of the trilogy. I will also go into detail and explain several theories I have about how important angelic ministry was to Christ as He walked upon the earth as an ordinary Man.

In addition to this, we will examine in much greater detail several keys to activating angelic activity in your life that were not fully elaborated upon in the first book due to space constraints. We will devote a great deal of the second book of this trilogy to the subject of the role of the Holy Spirit and His involvement in helping people to access the realm of angels. We will also look at the role or ministry of the Holy Spirit in helping a person or a group of people to open the heavens over their lives. Open heavens are critical to understand and activate angelic activity and visitations in a person's life. I will share several powerful testimonies about the role that the Holy Spirit played in opening the heavens in my life. I will also share numerous testimonies of ordinary people who saw and experienced the effects of the open heavens. Some of these testimonies are extremely supernatural in nature and are illustrated in great detail. Many people find these testimonies not only fascinating, but helping them to understand how easy it is to actually "rend" or rip open the heavens over their lives too. You could call this a "nuts and bolts" theology on open heavens in relation to angelic visitations.

That is the beautiful thing about this trilogy—as people read these testimonies, they tend to begin to experience the same kinds of supernatural experiences. This is because of the scriptural principle found in Revelation. As the apostle John fell at the feet of an angel to worship him, the heavenly being warns him against angel worship (a recurring theme in this trilogy) and gives him this powerful prophetic promise:

> *See that you do not do that! I am your fellow servant, and of your brethren who have the testimony of Jesus. Worship God! For the testimony of Jesus is the spirit of prophecy* (Revelation 19:10).

Again, we understand that we are never to worship an angel. We are also told that angels are our co-slaves, or fellow servants who have the testimony of Jesus. Finally, we are told that a testimony of Jesus is the spirit of prophecy. So when people read these testimonies about the Lord and His angels, they can be potential prophetic promises for them to appropriate. That is one reason that so many people are being impacted so powerfully by this book.

This includes tapping into or activating the anointing of the Holy Spirit that is found in or under an open heaven. It is really quite easy. However, there have not been a lot of books or teachings on this subject matter up till now. These testimonies give the reader a simple step-by-step outline, or "Kingdom keys" that can help unlock the heavens over their lives. Jesus is the role model I use for this principle in the second book. We need to base our faith squarely upon Christ alone and the model He emulated for us. You will see how this dynamic of the Kingdom of Heaven unfolded in my life, and in the testimonies in the second book, it becomes clear that it is not something unobtainable for you. You will be inspired, and your faith will be built up to believe to receive the same kinds of supernatural experiences. You will begin to understand what an open heaven is and also how to rend the heavens over your own life. This will result in the anointing of the Holy Spirit multiplying within your sphere of influence, and eventually activating you to see and co-labor with God's angels as the Lord leads you.

At times, this will also result in the manifest blessings of God or the favor of the Lord emerging in your life. Learning to live under an open heaven can be life-changing. That is the goal of this trilogy—to help people grow into the very image of Christ Jesus and into the power or anointing of the Holy Spirit. One other small but important benefit of this is the ability to recognize and work with God's angels. I will look at the dynamic of an open heaven in great detail and share several dynamic testimonies of open heavens and how angels have manifested in these circumstances. Finally, I will share an important reason that the Lord is allowing ordinary people to access the supernatural realm and this kind of authority at this hour.

This has to do with the restoration of all things that is outlined in Acts 3. The Lord is moving upon the hearts of people to be transformed into the very image of Christ and into the power of the Holy Spirit. This is because He wants us to demonstrate His Kingdom and His Gospel with His power. These both come from the revelation knowledge that is released to a person who is living under an open heaven. Actually, it is the restoration or establishment of the priesthood of all believers, and we will look at this aspect and dynamic of opening the heavens over your life in the conclusion of the book.

The conclusion of this book will dovetail seamlessly into the subject matter of the third book of this trilogy. One aspect of the priesthood of all believers is understanding how to operate in the power of the Holy Spirit by living your life under an open heaven. Another aspect of the priesthood of all believers is realizing that Christ has given us an example to follow and that we are called to be priests after the order of Melchizedek, having free access into the realms of Heaven. There we will receive supernatural revelation that will empower us to demonstrate Christ's Kingdom with the anointing and power of the Holy Spirit. This is Christ's example for us. One small but important part of the priesthood of all believers is the God-given ability to pass through the heavens, just like Jesus, the Son of God, and freely obtain revelation knowledge there. We will relate simple ways for the reader to do just that as we define the role of the priesthood of all believers.

Finally, *Dancing With Angels 2* is a well-written, biblically based book. It builds upon the foundation laid in the first book of the trilogy and continues to enlighten the reader with additional understanding of angelic ministry. You will be encouraged and gain a lot of knowledge and understanding about God's angels and the role that angelic ministry will play in the coming days. Hopefully you will realize that angelic ministry is a normal part of Christ's Kingdom and walking with God. Angelic encounters are not something that should be looked at with fear and suspicion. We hope that you will no longer be paranoid of the paranormal aspects of the Kingdom of Heaven. Your life will be changed, and you will be empowered to live in the power and anointing of the Holy Spirit. You will discover many simple ways to loose angels and rend the heavens over your life. By doing so, you will begin to live in a much greater level of victory and power, which Christ purchased for you on the Cross.

Dancing With Angels 2 also gives you additional insights into hidden mysteries of Christ's Kingdom concerning angels and unlocks simple secrets that can activate anyone to interact, recognize, and work with the angels that are already busy around each of us.

I am in no way seeking to exalt myself; rather, I am just relating the experiences that I enjoyed pertaining to the angelic realm. My only goal is to exalt Jesus Christ and be obedient to what I believe is the Lord's leading to put this manuscript on paper. The Lord is also leading us to donate 90 percent of the net proceeds from this book to help ministries that are preaching the Gospel to the poor and helping to minister to widows and orphans. I do not understand it all, but I believe that He has a purpose for these writings. My prayer is that Jesus is exalted and that His Kingdom is furthered by these books. Perhaps these testimonies will serve as the springboard to launch you into the greater works that Jesus is calling you to. Or perhaps the principle of Revelation 19:10 will be birthed in your heart and you will have your faith established to experience these kinds of angelic encounters and rip open the heavens over your life. Perhaps you will have your faith birthed to receive your healing or miracle. Whatever God does through these books, I give to Him all the glory, honor, and praise, as He alone is worthy.

Chapter 1

ANGELS IN THE CANON OF SCRIPTURE

In my previous book, we studied in some detail the way Jesus Christ viewed angels and working with angels. Christ's worldview concerning angels is very clear. The Lord embraces angels and angelic ministry. In fact, Christ has promised us that He would return with His angels to reap the last great harvest (see Matt. 25:31). Perhaps we need to reevaluate our mindset about angels too and approach heavenly angels in the same manner Jesus did. We should embrace angels and angelic ministry. We have allowed the fear of man and the fear of the unknown to paralyze us in our ability to interact with and activate angelic help. We should not be paranoid of the paranormal.

We should realize that Jesus has actually given ordinary people the power and authority to co-labor with His angelic hosts. We can work with angels, just as Jesus prophesies He will do in the coming days. After all, He has given to you and I all power and all authority to loose from Heaven and bind upon the earth (see Matt.

16:19; 28:18). Angels are our co-laborers who have the testimony of Christ. Christ's example encourages us to implement or activate angelic ministry and to utilize angelic help and intervention.

CHRIST'S EXAMPLE

Certainly Jesus not only believed in the ministry of angels but was aware He could employ them if He wished to do so. Jesus states:

> *Do you think that I cannot now pray to My Father, and He will provide Me with more than twelve legions of angels?* (Matthew 26:53)

In this passage, Jesus illustrated two of the most important keys to activate and release angelic ministry. Jesus tells us that He has the *authority* to *pray* to His Father. Jesus has given us this identical spiritual authority too.

It is almost certain that Jesus used His authority to loose angels and angelic ministry frequently in His life and ministry. Angels played a crucial and key role throughout the life and ministry of Christ while He walked the earth as a Man. Jesus also instructed His disciples (that is, you and me) how to pray. He promises us that He will do anything we ask and instructs us that we, also, have the authority to pray to the Father just like Him (see John 14:13; 16:24-27). The Lord taught and spoke about the reality of angelic ministry more than He taught about many of the modern Church's most accepted doctrines and pillars of faith. This would include doctrines like tithing, alms, the structure of the church, regular church attendance, church buildings, kid's church, Sunday school classes, missions, and the role of pastors or teachers, to name just a few. We need to begin to understand the legitimacy of angelic ministry in the Kingdom of God and how we are authorized to employ or loose angels just like our Savior. After all, Christ *is* our example (see Phil. 2:5; John 13:15; 1 Pet. 2:21; 1 John 2:6).

We have been given the authority to pray to our Father and ask for Him to release 12 legions of angels to help us in our times of need! By the way, 12 legions of angels are equal to 72,000 individual angels! I routinely pray for 12 legions of angels to encamp around our home. As simple as this principle sounds, many "have not" because they do not ask. We have been given permission by Jesus to pray and ask in His name. *Ask!* I often ask for the Lord to release and empower His angelic host to protect, guard, and guide us in our daily activities (see Matt. 7:7).

Let's look at this principle in Revelation 19:10, as this Scripture illustrates this concept clearly:

> *I fell at his feet* [an angel] *to worship him. But he* [an angel] *said to me, "See that you do not do that! I am your fellow servant, and of your brethren who have the testimony of Jesus. Worship God! For the testimony of Jesus is the spirit of prophecy."*

In this passage, we see that one of God's angels tells us that he is our fellow *servant*. The word the Bible uses for *servant* here is the Greek word *sundoulos*. *Sundoulos* can be translated as a co-slave (that is, servitor or ministrant of the same master, human or divine); a fellow servant, denoting union (or to work with, work together with, or work by association with or in unity with); companionship, process, resemblance, possession, instrumentality, addition; to work beside or in proximity with.[1] In compounds, it has similar applications, including completeness. The angel also tells us to *worship God,* not angels like him!

Clearly angels recognize that they are meant to work *with* us, *together* with us, or in *association* or *unity* with us, the Lord's children. In my earlier book, I stated how I had seen angels that become excited when we are allowed to see them, but angels become ecstatic when we begin to loose them and send them on missions of mercy in the realms of earth. I want to encourage you to read *Dancing with Angels 1: How to Work With Angels in Your Life* for a much more detailed examination of this subject. We have established that Jesus continues to work with angels to meet people's needs today, and Jesus will employ angels to fulfill His end-time mandates upon the earth. Let's continue to build upon this foundation by a brief examination of the role or duties of our co-laborers—angels—in the Scriptures.

THE ANGEL OF THE LORD

The Bible mentions about 300 specific references to the word "angel" or "angels." The first mention of an angel in the Bible is found in the book of Genesis. Let's look at Genesis 16:7: *"Now the Angel of the LORD found her by a spring of water in the wilderness...."* In this instance, the angel of the Lord came to Hagar. Incidentally, many biblical scholars believe that the *"Angel of the Lord"* in the Old Testament refers to Jesus. The term for this is *theophany,* which is defined as a manifestation of the Lord Jesus before His incarnation as a bodily human being. A theophany can also be defined as the appearance of Christ in the form of an angel.

This is one of the first examples, or the first mention, of angelic ministry in the Bible. I am omitting the reference in Genesis 3:24 in which the Lord assigned cherubim at the east of the Garden of Eden with a flaming sword to protect the tree of life. Here in Genesis 16 we see the angel of the Lord releasing divine direction, encouragement, and a prophetic word about an unborn child in Genesis 16:10-14. We should also notice that Hagar testifies that she has "seen" or "seen the back of" the angel of the Lord. Perhaps the angel was released in answer to her prayers; however, that is not clearly spelled out in this passage of Scripture. As we have learned previously, angels are sent in response to people's prayers and fasting. We will look at some of those examples in more detail later.

Hagar had an open-eyed encounter with an angelic being who prophesied over her unborn child. It is apparent that the angel walked right up to her at the well, and she carried on a conversation with him. Angels frequently speak (either in audible or unspoken words) prophetically to people who encounter them. He told her what to name her child (Ishmael) and also prophesied his destiny. This is an instance of an angel being sent directly from Heaven to seal, protect, and perform the word of the Lord and to speak a promise given by God Almighty. You can find that promise or word the angel was protecting in the blessings of Abraham (see Gen. 12). It is worth noting that the prophecy spoken by the angel of the Lord to Hagar was completely fulfilled. The descendants of Ishmael are still alive and well in the Arab and Muslim nations of the Middle East and throughout the entire world.

At times, the Lord uses angels to confirm His word and call upon an individual's life. I believe that we are entering into a new season of increased angelic activity of this nature. Many of God's champions, whom He is raising up at this hour to preach the Gospel, will encounter heavenly angels to confirm and establish their call. An example of this type of angelic ministry can be found in the life of Gideon (see Judg. 6:11-12). God employed an angel to commission Gideon into the ministry and his call to influence the destiny of Israel.

Going back to our first mention of angels, it is also interesting to note that Hagar was not a Hebrew but an Egyptian. Certainly, this means that the angels of God can appear to non-believers as well as believers. Another example of angelic visitation or ministry to non-Christians is found in Acts 10. Here we see that Cornelius, a Roman, has an encounter with an angel in direct response to his prayer, fasting, and gifts or alms to the poor. Again, the combination of these three spiritual tools seems to accelerate one's ability to see or discern angels and release angelic visitations in an individual's life.

In Acts 10, we discover that Cornelius clearly sees an angel with his natural eyes early in the morning. Like many humans who encounter an angel, Cornelius was afraid (see Acts 10:3-7). This angel speaks to Cornelius, clearly giving him divine direction, and Cornelius answers and interacts with the angelic messenger, asking him a question. According to the angel's divine instructions, he sends for the apostle Peter. It is interesting to note that the angel would not preach the Gospel to Cornelius, but rather instructed Cornelius to send for a human to preach the message of Christ Jesus. This is the wondrous work of the Sovereign Lord that He would depend upon weak humans to preach the glorious Gospel to the unsaved.

Simultaneously, as the result of a trance, Peter comes willingly to his home to share the Gospel of Jesus Christ. He made the way of salvation through faith in the death, burial, and resurrection of Jesus Christ known to Cornelius' entire Gentile household and friends. In addition to receiving salvation, these Gentiles were all filled with the Holy Spirit and spoke in tongues. Of course, in the Jewish culture and Law of Moses, Peter would have been strictly forbidden to have contact or interaction with such Gentiles in this manner. Perhaps some of our family members could benefit from this kind of angelic ministry leading to their salvation today?

It is very important to note that angels are not only mentioned but also play an extremely key role throughout the Bible from Genesis to Revelation. In fact, much of the Book of Revelation is based upon an angelic encounter that the apostle John experienced on the island of Patmos. It is truly awesome that God would use angelic ministry to visit the elderly apostle John to release the Book of Revelation to us. Again, we find that as a result of John's prayer, as he was *"in the Spirit"* on the Lord's day, there is a release of a supernatural visitation, which in turn gives the entire world a revelation of the mind of Christ (see Rev. 1:10). Much of the Book of Revelation was imparted to John with the help of angels.

Do you think that it may be important that some of the last words recorded by Jesus Christ in the Bible refer to His angel and His heritage? Look at Revelation 22:16:

> *I, Jesus, have sent **My angel** to testify to you these things in the churches. I am the Root and the Offspring of David, the Bright and Morning Star (emphasis mine).*

This is the last mention of angels in the Bible. Perhaps the fact that the Messiah clearly states He is sending His angel to the churches to speak to us may be important. This passage of Scripture clearly illustrates that Jesus has angels assigned to His command and His ongoing ministry upon the earth. God is still sending His angels into the earthly realm to speak to us today. There is no question about this fact. It might be wise for us to position ourselves to receive His servants and our fellow workers with clean hands, pure hearts, and open minds.

We will continue to explore the biblical aspects of angelic ministry throughout this book. By continuing to build upon a solid biblical foundation, we will keep on learning more facets about the nature of angelic ministry. We will look at numerous angelic encounters that have taken place over the years. The Lord of Hosts is releasing untold numbers of angels into the earth today that are being sent forth to minister to people's needs.

An important tool God has placed at our disposal is the ministry of angels. We need to open our eyes and hearts to be aware of these agents of revival. It is to our benefit that we learn how to biblically employ our angelic friends and fellow servants to accomplish God's call upon our lives and to live victoriously in this critical hour. My prayer is that this book, and the testimonies contained in it, will help launch many into the reality of our supernatural God and angelic encounters.

I would like to state this fact as clearly and as distinctly as possible. Jesus Christ must be the absolute central focus of our relationship with God. We are to worship God. The resurrection of the Lord Jesus Christ and His finished work on the Cross of Calvary must be the absolute cornerstone of our faith. God is a triune or three-part Being composed of God the Father, God the Son, and God the Holy Spirit. We are instructed to worship God alone. As such, we should personally invest our time in worship of all three parts of the Godhead. The Bible plainly instructs believers to worship God. Angel worship or adoration is strictly forbidden in Scripture (see Luke 4:7-8; Gal. 1:8).

In the next chapter, I will continue building upon the foundation of Christ by taking a more in-depth look at how angels ministered to Christ while He walked upon the earth as a mortal Man.

ENDNOTES

1. Strong, James. *Strong's Exhaustive Concordance of the Bible.* Peabody, MA: Hendrickson

Chapter 2

A CLOSER LOOK AT ANGELS IN THE LIFE OF CHRIST

In my previous book, I touched on the concept of how angels did in fact minister to Christ Jesus. I would like to take the liberty to elaborate and expand upon Christ's angelic visitations. As we have touched upon previously, angels are used by God to meet people's immediate needs and also to answer their prayers, which most times coincide. Hebrews illustrates this ministry of angels (see also Ps. 103:20).

> *Of* the angels He [God] *says: "Who makes His angels spirits and His ministers a flame of fire." ...Are they* [God's angels] *not all ministering spirits sent forth to minister for those who will inherit salvation?* (Hebrews 1:7,14)

The language used in Hebrews 1:14 concerning the *spirits sent to serve* seems to indicate that angels are sent to help an individual in the same manner a waiter would serve you a meal in a fine res-taurant. In other words, angels are created to be at your "beck and call." The Greek word used here for *serve* is *diakonia* and can be translated as "to be in *attendance* to an individual (like a servant); to offer *aid*, or an (official) *service*, or to *help* one by giving or min-istering aid, relief, or a needed service."[1] The parabolic meaning is clear. At times, the Lord will utilize or allow individuals to *activate* angels to serve them or others as required to facilitate an important desire or immediate need.

A good analogy of this dynamic of angelic ministry could be described in this way. Angels serve people in the same way that your favorite waiter would serve you your favorite meal to celebrate your birthday in your favorite restaurant. This aspect or dynamic of angelic ministry speaks of favor with both God and His angelic hosts. If you take the time to think about it, you will find that it is quite comforting to perceive angels in this light. God's angels are our co-laborers that are willing, ready, and able to serve us in any way necessary!

Jesus understood this fact! When we comprehend this dynamic of how angels interact with us, it can revolutionize our lives! Again, we should not be paranoid of the paranormal aspects of the Messiah's Kingdom. A significant method that heavenly angels ministered to Christ as a mortal Man was through answering His prayers in the Hebrews 1:14 model. Please keep in mind that Jesus Christ was a flesh and blood human being just like you and I (see Heb. 2:18; 4:15; 5:7-9). However, it is important to remember that angels can be empowered by God to manifest the answers to the prayers of believers and non-believers alike, and the Scriptures seem to indicate that angels were sent in answer to Jesus' prayers too.

MINISTRY TO JESUS

A careful study of the Scriptures reveals that angels were employed to minister to Jesus numerous times. Angels certainly strengthened the Lord in His time of need on more than one occasion. It appears the angels ministered to the Lord Jesus as a result of His prayers or possibly as an answer to His prayers. Perhaps as Jesus prayed to His Father, our Father responded to His only begotten Son on earth by releasing angels from the realms of Heaven to minister to Jesus' needs. Luke bears out this concept: *"Then an angel appeared to Him* [Jesus] *from heaven, strengthening Him"* (Luke 22:43).

This passage is taken from the night that the Lord earnestly prayed in the Garden of Gethsemane. The Lord was well aware of what His fate was to be upon the Cross of Calvary. He prayed intensely, asking the Father to *"take this cup away"* from Him (see Luke 22:42). The Bible tells us that *"His sweat became like great drops of blood falling down to the ground"* (Luke 22:44). It is obvious that Christ was in mortal agony. Jesus knew that He would suffer a brutal, excruciatingly painful, and grisly death upon the Cross. It is possible that Christ's act of Passion on the Cross was the topic of discussion with Moses and Elijah on the Mount of Transfiguration (see Matt. 17:1-13). Jesus desperately wanted to be strengthened to endure the ordeal of bearing the weight of the sin of all humankind. In the heat of this defining moment and this divine ordeal, our Lord was Himself strengthened by angelic ministry. Yes, Christ was fully God, but He was also fully man. By the Lord's example, we can learn and begin to grow in the wisdom and knowledge necessary to loose angels in our times of need.

We see the angels also ministered to the Lord at the very beginning of His ministry. After the Lord was filled with the Holy Spirit, He was led by the Spirit into the wilderness and fasted for 40 days. During this period, Jesus was tempted. Once Jesus had successfully withstood the devil (for our sakes), the Bible tells us: *"When He* [Christ] *had fasted forty days and forty nights, afterward He was hungry"* (Matt. 4:2). It was at this point that multiple angels ministered to Jesus. We see that in Mark:

> *He was there in the wilderness forty days, tempted by Satan, and was with the wild beasts; and the angels ministered to Him* (Mark 1:13).

Did Jesus pray and release those angels? Did the angels actually minister to Jesus by giving Him some food? The Scriptures do not clearly spell this out, but it would seem logical that, since Jesus was alone in the desert, the angels ministered to Him by feeding Him. Also, since the Scripture mentions that Jesus *"was with the wild beasts,"* it is probable that the angels also acted to protect the Messiah during this time of vulnerability and need. As of this writing, I have traveled to Africa 22 times and have occasionally been in areas in or near game reserves and found myself unwillingly in a situation where I was with the wild beasts. In that instance, the Lord sent angels to help not only me but a large group of people with whom I was traveling.

However, it appears that angels ministered to Jesus while He was in the desert by meeting His immediate needs for nourishment and protection. Notice that the Scripture clearly illustrates that there was more than one angel. Perhaps this was an instance when 72,000 showed up and encamped around the mortal Christ! I believe they actually fed Jesus by giving Him food and water.

We also see a prophetic picture of this kind of angelic ministry illustrated in the life of Elijah. By the way, remember that the Lord rained manna to feed the children of Israel while they were in the desert (see Exod. 16). That is the very nature of our Father (see Gen. 22:8).

OUR PRAYERS

Let's consider this passage of Scripture from a personal perspective. If you had been on a 40-day fast and found yourself alone in the desert or the wilderness (this infers a long way from any civilization) and you had not eaten any food for 40 days, you would most likely be very weak and hungry. Let's imagine that you were in the middle of the Serengeti game reserve in the Rift Valley of East Africa. What would you do if there were wild beasts like lions and leopards in the area, even close by your location? I can say that at times I have been in these situations and have heard lions prowling nearby. This has actually happened to me; I began to pray very earnestly! There would be no Tim Horton's, McDonald's, or other place to buy food. You might call out to God to help you in prayer. We will also look at a biblical example of a young child who did so in just a moment.

I know personally my prayer would sound something like this: "Oh, Jesus! I am starving out here! Can I get a Big Mac or something? Maybe a Starbucks decaf cappuccino would help! Lord! I can hear the lions and hyenas nearby. Lord I need Your *help!*" So it is rational to think that perhaps Jesus, as a flesh and blood mortal, was surely a little hungry and perhaps somewhat concerned about the wild beasts, too, after His 40-day water fast. Look at what Hebrews tells us:

For we do not have a High Priest who cannot sympathize with our weaknesses, but was in all points tempted as we are, yet without sin (Hebrews 4:15).

Remember the deceiver had just tempted Jesus with food: *"If You are the Son of God, command that these stones become bread"* (Matt. 4:3). This confirms that Jesus was indeed hungry. The Scripture illustrates that angels have given bread to other people before Christ's time.

However, we can say with 100 percent certainty that Jesus was the benefactor of angelic ministry. To say it another way, Jesus had an angelic visitation, or angelic encounter, in the desert! In fact, Jesus saw and encountered more than one angel. Again, Scripture does not indicate the exact number. I believe that there were numerous angels that served the Son of God, but we do know without any doubt that there were at least two. Scripture confirms that God will, at times, send angels to minister to or serve people by supplying them food, water, or both, just like a waiter in a fine restaurant.

ELIJAH

There are other documented examples in the Bible where the Lord released angels to provide food or nourishment for individuals. Elijah is probably the most recognizable example. Look at First Kings:

Then as he lay and slept under a broom tree, suddenly an angel touched him, and said to him, "Arise and eat." Then he looked, and there by his head was a cake baked on coals, and a jar of water. So he ate and drank, and lay down again. And the angel of the LORD came back the second time, and touched him, and said, "Arise and eat,

*because the journey is too great for you." So he arose, and
ate and drank; and he went in the strength of that food
forty days and forty nights as far as Horeb, the mountain
of God* (1 Kings 19:5-8).

There are a few things to notice in this passage. First, Elijah
was about to go on a 40-day fast like the Lord Jesus. This is a principle, or key, that can help to unlock the unseen realm—fasting.
The angel gave the prophet food that sustained him for 40 days of
fasting and a very long journey. At times as we seek the Lord with
extended fasting and prayer, we will encounter angels. Remember,
fasting is an important key in activating angelic ministry at times,
and fasting is often associated with opening the eyes of a person to
see into the angelic realm and opening the heavens over our lives.
Fasting is a key.

In this biblical example of angelic ministry, we find that the
angel actually does feed the prophet. It has been reported that Iris
Ministries in East Africa is seeing the Lord release the creative
miracle of multiplying food for the orphans in their care. This is
the very nature of God (see Exod. 16:35). Of course, when the Lord
rained down manna from Heaven to feed the children of Israel in
the desert, it was also a prophetic picture of the life of Christ, who
is the Bread of Life. I wonder—did the angels of Heaven serve that
manna to the children of Israel?

This was not the only time that Elijah was fed supernaturally.
Look in First Kings 17:6: *"The ravens brought him bread and meat
in the morning, and bread and meat in the evening; and he drank
from the brook."* There is also the time that the widow and her son
were given a supernatural multiplication of provision (see 1 Kings
17:12-15). Scriptures do not give us insight into how the flour and

oil did not dry up, but I believe that it was the result of angelic intervention in the prophet's life once again. Perhaps an angel of provision multiplied the flour and oil each day? We have witnessed anointing oil multiply.

ANGELIC ACTIVITY

We are living in the day and hour when the Lord is releasing these kinds of miracles of provision to many people. At times, angels will be involved in this supernatural process. The Lord once supernaturally supplied me with strawberry freezer jam in a mystical way. I was alone in Kansas City in the middle of a "semi-Daniel fast" and was praying just prior to an extended trip to Tanzania in February of 2005. One morning, as I was eating toast, I finished the last jar of Kathy's homemade freezer jam. I was quite disappointed, as strawberry freezer jam was my little treat during my one meal a day. So I searched diligently throughout our freezer and actually emptied out everything it contained looking for a jar of strawberry freezer jam, but there was none left. (If you fast, you may understand the intensity of my search.)

I also searched the entire refrigerator section and at last sighed in disappointment and defeat. There was no more strawberry freezer jam to be had. So, vanquished, I uttered a little heart's prayer, "Lord, I wish I had more strawberry freezer jam for my fast," and I sulked into my prayer room. Of course, this is an obvious oxymoron! I was alone in the house. The next morning when I opened the refrigerator, guess what was sitting right in front on the top shelf? That is right—one fresh, unopened jar of strawberry freezer jam! This too, I believe, was the result of angelic ministry, as there had been no other human being in the house save for me!

In Genesis, we see that an angel was also dispatched from Heaven in response to a small child's prayer for provision, specifically water. Look at this passage:

> *The water in the skin was used up, and she placed the boy under one of the shrubs. Then she went and sat down across from him at a distance of about a bowshot; for she said to herself, "Let me not see the death of the boy." So she sat opposite him, and lifted her voice and wept. And God heard the voice of the lad. Then the angel of God called to Hagar out of heaven, and said to her, "What ails you, Hagar? Fear not, for God has heard the voice of the lad where he is"* (Genesis 21:15-17).

Notice it is the boy Ishmael's prayer that the Lord hears and responds to. Also notice that Hagar hears *"the angel of God,"* and then she sees the answer to her son's prayer manifest in the natural realm.

I want you to see a couple of points here. First, the Lord is no respecter of persons and will readily hear the prayers of children and respond by releasing angelic ministry. This is because the children have pure hearts (see Matt. 5:8). Second, Hagar heard, but did not see, the angel. Nonetheless, in this instance the manifestation of the angelic encounter was realized in the natural realm in the form of water and most likely saved the lives of Hagar and Ishmael.

At times we will *discern* an angel's presence and not see them but will realize the fruit of their visitation into our space—for example, when they drop off strawberry freezer jam. Look at verse 19 to see the manifestation of the angelic ministry:

Then God opened her eyes, and she saw a well of water.
And she went and filled the skin with water, and gave the
lad a drink (Genesis 21:19).

This also illustrates that the Lord used an angel to protect the prophetic word that the Lord had spoken over Abraham's son Ishmael. God still uses angels to provide for and protect His children today, just like we saw illustrated in the life of Christ.

Having said all of this, it is safe to speculate that the amount of angelic activity in the life of Jesus Christ was immense. Most likely, the number of angelic visitations and encounters that Jesus Christ experienced in His life were much more pronounced and dramatic than are outlined for us in the canon of Scripture. Of course, you may say that this is extra-biblical. I pray that you will have the opportunity to ask one of Christ's angels or perhaps the Lord Himself. Remember that if you are seeking to go to Heaven when you die, you are seeking to spend eternity in the company of an innumerable multitude of angels! And again, with over 100 references to angels in the New Testament alone, it is certain that angels are an integral part of the Kingdom of God!

Christ still implements and makes use of angels and angelic ministry to accomplish His mandates upon the earth and in the lives of ordinary people today. That should be exciting news to everyone who is reading this now. It is apparent that the Lord still uses angels in this fashion today and will certainly continue to multiply this kind of angelic intervention in the lives of His people as the world grows darker and more perverse. Now let's begin to add additional scriptural insights concerning angelic ministry to our growing foundation as we journey through the coming pages and examine the amazing personal testimonies of angelic visitations ahead. We will also begin to examine the importance of the phenomenon called "open heavens" in the subsequent chapters, and we will discover the importance of open heavens to angelic visitations. In the next chapter, we will see how Christ Himself opened the heavens for humankind.

ENDNOTE

1. Strong, James. *Strong's Exhaustive Concordance of the Bible.* Peabody, MA: Hendrickson Publishers, 2007. #G1248.

Chapter 3

JESUS AND OPEN HEAVENS

We have seen from examination of Christ's life that He enjoyed a wealth of angelic intervention and visitations while He walked upon the earth. This fact begs the question—why? As we have learned, the Lord was fully God, but He was also fully Man with a nature just like ours, yet without sin. Jesus needed to eat, to rest, and to seek a relationship with His Father. Christ was divine, but He was also fully Man. So how can we explain the abundance of angelic activity in the Lord's earthly life?

One answer to this question is found in Luke:

> *When all the people were baptized, it came to pass that Jesus also was baptized; and while He prayed, the heaven was opened. And the Holy Spirit descended in bodily form like a dove upon Him, and a voice came from heaven which said, "You are My beloved Son; in You I am well pleased" (Luke 3:21-22).*

What a powerful portrait of the love of the Father and the freedom that Christ had to enter into the realms of Heaven or the spirit. This incident marks the first time that all three parts of the Godhead were together in unity upon the earth for the benefit of mankind since the Garden of Eden. Therefore, this incident has a very important and substantial parabolic significance. In Eden, humankind walked under an open heaven on a continual basis, and there was no interruption in the communion that Adam and Eve had with the Godhead. They saw God clearly. They heard God clearly. In February of 2010, Kathy had a vision that further illustrates this point.

VISION OF THE GARDEN OF EDEN

I was in a beautiful garden of trees and shrubs that were lush and a beautiful green. The leaves of the trees were big and very healthy. There were no dying trees or brown leaves like we see here on earth; everything was breathtakingly beautiful. The garden was dark, like night time, but still the garden was pristine and lovely. I also noticed a beautiful, warm light illuminating around where I was standing and looked over to my right and saw an enormous shaft or portal of light coming down from Heaven. It was then I realized I was in the Garden of Eden.

I was so amazed at the portal of light that I went over and stood directly under it and looked up. It was truly beautiful. It shimmered with a white light that we do not see here on earth. It glimmered with shimmering gold, pearl, and diamond rays of light with very light, soft colors of red, blue, and green, like colors of a rainbow, and the light was very dense or thick with the glory of God. It glistened and looked alive and active. The portal was very close to the ground, about 15 feet above my head, and I saw a ring of God's glory fire around the opening of the portal. I realized that the light contained God and was God.

Everything of God was in the light, and it was so spectacular that I could not take my eyes off of it. The light was very bright, but it did not hurt my eyes as I gazed up into it and I could see eternally forever. There was incredible love, peace, joy, and rest in there, and I knew that God and His angels descended and ascended back up into Heaven in the portal. I knew that the Garden of Eden and Heaven were one, just like God the Father, God the Son, and God the Holy Spirit are three Persons but they are One. The light that came down from Heaven was holy, righteous, and pure. I did not see any activity, though.

I kept looking to see if God the Father, God the Son, and God the Holy Spirit would come down. I kept looking for a while but saw no one, and I was very sad and my heart was grieved. As a result of this vision, I believe that we can actually live out the Lord's Prayer on earth today. *"Our Father in heaven, hallowed be Your name. Your kingdom come. Your will be done on earth as it is in heaven."*

I believe this prayer. I believe we can have God's Kingdom here on earth. I believe that Heaven and earth can be one on this earth, that we can have all of Heaven here on earth. I believe we can walk blamelessly here on earth before the Lord, just as Jesus walked here on earth, but in my vision the Garden of Eden was dark. There was not any activity in the portal. I believe that aspect of the vision represents this time. The Church does not believe the Lord's Prayer. The Church does not believe that His Kingdom and His will can be done on earth as it is in Heaven. Much of the Church does not believe that angels are for today, or that the fullness of His power, miracles, healings, and the gifts of the Spirit are for today.

In the vision, the Garden was dark but still beautiful, lush, green, healthy, and strong, which means *we can still have it!* God is waiting for us, but we need to become like Him through the open heavens! The Bible says that after the fall of Adam and Eve, we were born with a sin nature, we are all sinful, but Jesus was born of a woman (of sinful nature) yet He did not sin and walked blamelessly before His Father with no sin, which means we can do the same. Jesus' life on earth was an example for us here on earth to follow. How can we do this? We need to walk like Jesus; we need to be like Jesus in every way. Just as Jesus was like His Father, we need to be like Him!

The Garden of Eden represents communion and intimacy with God on a daily basis—every hour, minute, and second of the day being just like Jesus in every way. Darkness in the Garden represents unbelief—no communion or intimacy. The portal represents, *"Your kingdom come. Your will be done on earth as it is in heaven"* in our hearts. No activity in the portal or open heavens of the vision is parabolic, or symbolic of the fact that most people do not accept the things of God or heavenly things like angels, gifts of the Spirit, and the power and anointing of the Holy Spirit.

However, God wants to restore these heavenly treasures to us in this hour.

Adam and Eve had uninterrupted communion or fellowship with God eternally in Eden. They lived under an open heaven. Christ came to restore humankind to our rightful place of living under an open heaven in constant communion and friendship with God. This was one of Christ's primary missions. Jesus Christ came to reinstate this dynamic of perpetual relationship between God and humanity. This process will accelerate because the Lord is opening heavens for His children at this hour. Jesus modeled how we can access or open the heavens over our lives.

OPENING THE HEAVENS

As Jesus prayed on the day that He was baptized, the heavens opened over His life. The result was that Christ began His ministry under an open heaven and operated under an open heaven from that day forward. Luke 3:23 tells us, *"Now Jesus Himself began His ministry at about thirty years of age...."* So we understand that there was a God-ordained moment of time that the Father had predetermined to open the heavens over Jesus and consequently re-opened the heavens over His creation, humankind. This was the beginning of ministry in His life.

Jesus benefited from the open heavens over His life throughout His earthly ministry. It was the open heavens that Jesus ministered under that helped prepare Him and empower Him to manifest the Kingdom of God at various times and places. Living under an open heavens is not only possible, but it is also imperative for you and me today.

We also need to understand that God is the One who is responsible for opening the heavens over a person's life. This is the sovereign work of the Holy Spirit. Remember, we have learned that Jesus is indeed our role model and that He has given us an example to follow (see John 13:15; Phil. 2:5; 1 Pet. 2:21; 1 John 2:6). Jesus came to earth to break open the heavenly realms for us all. That was a critical aspect of Christ's call and mission. He came to give you and me power and authority. Let me encourage you that one of the most important things that Jesus gave you and I all power and authority to accomplish was to open the heavens over our lives and over our spheres of influence. We can accomplish this just like Jesus did with our prayers and acts of repentance. We all need Christ's total salvation in every aspect of our lives. This includes the restoration of the open heavens over our lives.

So looking at this passage of Scripture, we see some important keys to opening the heavens. We see that the heavens opened over Jesus as He was baptized and while He prayed. Therefore, we should also seek to be baptized and also to pray like Christ. Baptism is symbolic of repentance of sin. The Scriptures do not tell us what kind of prayer Jesus prayed as He was baptized. However, I am certain that He prayed for the heavens to be opened. This is perhaps the most important key to opening the heavens over your life: prayer. Jesus gave us the authority to ask the Father for open heavens in His name (see John 16:23).

We also see that Jesus began His ministry after the heavens opened over His life. When the heavens opened over the Lord, we see that there was immediate fruit or manifestations of God's Kingdom. The first thing that is apparent in the open heaven that is now over Christ's life is the visible manifestation of the Holy Spirit descending in the bodily form of a dove. Miracles, signs, and wonders abounded in the open heaven that opened over Jesus that day. What is really being described in this passage is this: The corporate anointing to see into the spiritual realm was released, and people saw the Holy Spirit manifest in a tangible form as a dove. In Chapter 12, we will look at a modern-day testimony of Heaven opening in a similar manner where the Holy Spirit actually descended into a church in the form of a dove in 2005.

When the heavens opened over Jesus, the gift of discerning of spirits was activated and the people saw into the spiritual realm. This is the fruit of an open heaven. We also see that the people had their spiritual ears open to hear the Father speak in an audible voice, saying, *"You are My beloved Son; in You I am well pleased."* You will note that the Father was speaking to Jesus, but because of the open heaven that was over Christ at that moment, many of the people present both saw and heard into and from the spiritual realm. They entered into the spirit by proximity. They heard God. They saw God just like in the Garden of Eden. It is critical that we hear God clearly in this season. And that is why it is absolutely necessary that we seek to open the heavens over our lives and sphere of influence. We need to hear God clearly. We need to see what God is doing clearly. These two things are imperative, and we can accomplish them in a much more effective way when we get the heavens open over our lives. Remember that Jesus only did those things that He saw His Father doing (see John 5:19).

Peter, James, and John witnessed Jesus' baptism and the supernatural phenomenon that accompanied this event. (See Luke 3:20-24.) They also witnessed the fruit of the open heaven that was continuously over Jesus on several other occasions. In Acts 4:20, they told the religious leaders—who could have well crucified them—this: *"For we cannot but speak the things which we have seen and heard."* One of the things they had seen and heard was the voice of the Father and the appearance of the Holy Spirit.

ON EARTH AS IT IS IN HEAVEN

It is important that we understand that there are certain characteristics of an open heaven that we can still benefit from today. Primarily, these include the ability to recognize heavenly things and to both see and hear from the realms of Heaven or the spirit. Both of these benefits are absolutely critical if we are to fulfill the mandate of Matthew 6:10 and pray like Jesus prays: *"Your kingdom come. Your will be done on earth as it is in heaven."* We can also experience the supernatural unction of the Holy Spirit when we live under open heavens (see 1 John 2:20). Open heavens give us the ability to see, hear, and receive supernatural revelations from the Kingdom of Heaven. We need all of these in the hour in which we live. Of course, the gifting to *see* angels is also the fruit of an open heaven.

In order for us to release God's Kingdom upon the earth in the same manner that the Kingdom exists in Heaven, it is absolutely necessary for us to both see and hear from Heaven clearly. We need to have the unction of the Holy Spirit and supernatural revelation of all things. These three things were absolutely necessary for Jesus, too. That is why He did not begin His ministry until the heavens were opened over Him. Jesus operated under an open heaven for the remainder of His earthly life. We will see from a careful study of the Scriptures that there were many times that other people were impacted by the open heaven that was manifested that day when Jesus began His ministry at the age of about 30. Let's begin to look at a few examples where the open heaven that was upon, within, or over Jesus impacted other people.

When the heavens opened over Jesus, people saw and heard into the spirit. At times these ordinary people saw and heard angels.

This dynamic of open heavens is still true today. When you find an individual or a geographic location where the heavens are open, you will often discover angelic activity and movement. Again, a simple prayer in these places and circumstances can activate the eyes of your heart or spirit to perceive the angelic activity that is unfolding around you.

We see this principle unfold in the lives of Peter, James, and John in Matthew. Look at this passage that is commonly referred to as the Mount of Transfiguration:

> *Now after six days Jesus took Peter, James, and John his brother, led them up on a high mountain by themselves; and He was transfigured before them. His face shone like the sun, and His clothes became as white as the light. And behold, Moses and Elijah appeared to them, talking with Him. Then Peter answered and said to Jesus, "Lord, it is good for us to be here; if You wish, let us make here three tabernacles: one for You, one for Moses, and one for Elijah." While he was still speaking, behold, a bright cloud overshadowed them; and suddenly a voice came out of the cloud, saying, "This is My beloved Son, in whom I am well pleased. Hear Him!" And when the disciples heard it, they fell on their faces and were greatly afraid. But Jesus came and touched them and said, "Arise, and do not be afraid"* (Matthew 17:1-7).

Let's look at several aspects of this powerful event. First, what we actually see is the three disciples of Christ stepping into the spirit because of the open heaven that was upon Jesus. So what this passage really describes is an open heaven encounter. Notice that it was a specific time. This dynamic was also in operation in the first instance of an open heaven that we saw in Luke 3. Timing is critical to opening the heavens over your life. When the disciples saw Christ transfigured, they were really seeing into the spiritual realm. Of course this was a supernatural event, but we could also accurately define this experience by saying that the disciples had the gift of discerning of spirits activated in their lives. Also note that Jesus took the three disciples to a specific geographic location at a fixed or appointed time. Again, these are important keys to opening the heavens over your life. The disciples entered into the spirit by proximity yet again.

The activation or impartation of the gift of discerning of spirits is often the fruit or outcome that unfolds in a person's life when he or she enters into or experiences an open heaven. Remember that the gift of discerning of spirits is the supernatural ability and gift of the Holy Spirit to see, smell, hear, and perceive spiritual beings—both angelic beings and demonic beings. The gift of discerning of spirits is also the ability to recognize elements or aspects of the spirit or heavenly places. That is what is happening here with Peter, James, and John; they see into the spirit and hear the voice of God. This is the second time they hear the Father. Only this time there is a significant difference. The Father speaks directly to the disciples and tells them to listen to Jesus! When you rip open the heavens over your life, the Father will speak directly to you, too. Most likely He will tell you the same thing! *"Hear Him!"*

The disciples also see Moses and Elijah talking to Jesus. Did you ever wonder how the three disciples knew that they were seeing Moses and Elijah? Obviously they had never met them, seen their portraits, or searched out their likeness on the Internet. So again we see that this supernatural revelation was the fruit of experiencing the open heaven that was upon the Lord. The disciples began to operate in the unction of the Holy Spirit, and they knew all things. This is the manifestation of the spirit of wisdom and revelation (see Isa. 11:2; 1 John 2:20). That is another great benefit to opening the heavens over your life. Now let's take this a step further. We know from the Scriptures that Elijah was transported into the very presence of God, or Heaven (see 2 Kings 2:11). So therefore, it is very plausible that the three men were seeing into the realms of Heaven at that moment. Again, this is the fruit of an open heaven.

The disciples also saw Moses, who was carrying on a conversation with Jesus. Briefly, let me say that the three were discussing Christ's divine destiny upon the tree of Calvary, but that is really the material of another book. I only suggest it to you here for your edification and further study. Now we know that Moses died at the age of 120 (see Deut. 34:5-7). Therefore, the disciples saw Jesus speaking to Moses who was dead. Was Christ communing with the dead or practicing necromancy? Of course not! However, this biblical example of the Lord speaking to a dead man begs some explanation.

We can rightly say that Moses was at that moment of time receiving the answer to his prayer found in Exodus 33:18 when He asked God this question: *"Please, show me Your glory."* On the other hand, Moses was dead. We know that Moses' body was buried (see Deut. 34:6). So was it really Moses that was speaking to Christ, or was it Moses' spirit man? Yes, it was Moses and Elijah who the disciples saw taking counsel with Christ. So we could accurately say that Moses was at the moment of this conversation a member of the great cloud of witnesses (see Heb. 12:1). So once again we find that the disciples had their spiritual senses activated to see into the realm of the spirit. And a case could be made to say that Peter, James, and John saw the spirit or angel of Moses. I submit this theory to you for study. It is not important to our quest; however, it does confirm the point that under the open heaven that was upon Jesus, the men saw spiritual beings or saw into the spirit. Again, this is one of the primary benefits of open heavens. Often, when you are in a place where the heavens are open, you will see angels. Let's look at a few more examples in Scripture.

Luke 24 provides a great example of bumping into angels in a place where the heavens had opened:

> *Now on the first day of the week, very early in the morning, they, and certain other women with them, came to the tomb bringing the spices which they had prepared. But they found the stone rolled away from the tomb. Then they went in and did not find the body of the Lord Jesus. And it happened, as they were greatly perplexed about this, that behold, two men stood by them in shining garments. Then, as they were afraid and bowed their faces to the earth, they said to them, "Why do you seek the living among the dead? He is not here, but is risen! Remember how He spoke to you when He was still in Galilee, saying, 'The Son of Man must be delivered into the hands of sinful men, and be crucified, and the third day rise again.'" And they remembered His words* (Luke 24:1-8).

Certainly on that resurrection morn the heavens were open at the tomb of Christ. The women were the beneficiaries of an angelic visitation. Again we see the characteristics of open heavens manifest in this instance. These are just ordinary women, but when they step into the geographic area where the open heaven that was upon the Lord was still lingering, they both saw and heard into the spiritual realm. The result was that they saw the angels that were present. They also were given a prophecy or message by the two angelic beings. This, of course, is the very definition of an angel. Angels bring or relate messages or revelations from the Lord. Finally, the end result was that they had the unction of the Holy Spirit manifest, and they were given a supernatural knowledge or revelation of Christ as the Messiah.

The ascension is another powerful example of how the open heavens that were upon Christ impacted those who were in the same geographic area. We will look at this illustration of open heavens in Chapter 6. Again, it is important to remember that the Lord can send you to a geographic area or specific place where the heavens are already open to help activate or open the heavens over your life. We have seen this dynamic unfold in my testimony and life. Perhaps the Lord will use a similar pattern in your life. So allow me to encourage you to be obedient to the leadings of the Holy Spirit when you are asked to travel to a new place.

MAHANAIM

Perhaps the Lord has a purpose for such a trip, and it could be something that God requires of you. Your obedience to take such a trip could turn out to be your Mount of Transfiguration experience. We have called these prophetic acts of obedience. Search for places or geographic areas that are under an open heaven. There are lots of places like this on the earth today. I call these areas a Mahanaim. That simply means a place where God is present. Genesis 32:2 illustrates this concept: *"When Jacob saw them [angels], he said, 'This is God's camp.' And he called the name of that place Mahanaim."* Jacob found himself in a place where he experienced an angelic visitation. These places are still around today, and you can find them. Let me encourage you to search them out.

The disciples of Jesus were present when the heavens initially opened over the Lord on the day He was baptized in Luke 3:22. They saw and heard from the spiritual realm because of the open heaven that was upon Jesus. They experienced Christ's open heaven at the Mount of Transfiguration. They were also present when the heavens opened over Christ at His ascension. Jesus carried an open heaven within or upon Himself. That can be true of friends of God today, too.

We should remember that the heavens can be open over an individual as well as a specific geographical area or location. Again, Jesus is our scriptural example for this principle concerning the dynamic of open heavens and how to enter into them by proxy. So the Lord may lead you to submit to the ministry of a specific individual who is operating in or under an open heaven. We need to understand that certain individuals carry open heavens with them everywhere they go. You could say the fragrance of Heaven is attached to a person who is living under an open heaven. You may learn from them or from their teaching materials. You may wish to consider attending events where these folks are ministering. If possible, seek opportunities to interact with them on a personal basis and ask them questions. People call this discipleship, but I prefer to call this kind of interaction friendship. The Lord used Kenneth E. Hagin to encourage and help disciple me in my early walk in the supernatural. Although I was not able to have a personal friendship with him, I was able to learn from Hagin's books and audio teachings. The Lord also used the ministry of Benny Hinn in a similar way in my life. Ask the Holy Spirit to guide you and give you direction in this area.

When the heavens are open over a person or place, people will often see and hear from the realms of Heaven or the spirit by proximity. You will garner supernatural revelations in such a place. We have seen this from our scriptural examples. This dynamic or characteristic of open heavens is still in effect today. So I encourage you to find a place, individual, or ministry that is moving under an open heaven and then seek to invest as much time as you can in that environment. When you enter into the proximity of an open heaven, you will at times begin to see and hear angels. At this point, you are in a position to begin to exercise your spiritual senses. We need to build spiritual senses up according to the principle of Hebrews 5:14:

> *Solid food belongs to those who are of full age, that is, those who **by reason of use have their senses exercised to discern** both good and evil (emphasis mine).*

There are some folks who will not stay too long in Moravian Falls because they get too much revelation and are not able to sleep properly.

In conclusion, let me encourage you to seek the Lord for direction and guidance. The Holy Spirit will guide you and teach you the best methods and manner to rend the heavens over your life. You should not be in a hurry, nor should you be fixated on any one avenue to rip or rend the heavens over your life. Allow the Lord to guide your steps. Some folks are not interested in traveling or ministry. God is so wonderful and kind that He gives each of us a choice of how we live out our lives. You can choose to live a "normal" life without the miracles, signs, wonders, and angelic interaction that manifest in an open heaven.

However, you will benefit immensely from living your life under an open heaven as the blessings of Abraham will manifest in your life. The fruit of an open heaven over your life is favor, blessing, revelation, and the release of the power, gifting, and anointing of the Holy Spirit upon you and all that you put your hand to. You will just prosper! So I want to encourage you to rend the heavens over your life. Let's investigate several supernatural events that helped open the heavens over my life through the guidance and ministry of the Holy Spirit in the next chapter. These testimonies will illustrate what it might look like when the Lord leads you to open the heavens over your life. Finally, we need to remember that it is only through the finished work of Jesus Christ that we can rend or rip open the heavens over our lives. Christ came to rend or open the heavens for all of humankind. Jesus accomplished this by His finished work on the Cross of Calvary. Therefore, we can all live under an open heaven today.

Chapter 4

THE HOLY SPIRIT AND OPEN HEAVENS

In my previous book, I described a parabolic experience that I walked through in the city of Botwood, Newfoundland, Canada. That morning, Thursday, November 29, 2001, was the morning that the Holy Spirit invited me to go for a walk with Him in the cool of the day. That experience is related to the reader in great detail in Chapter 5 of *Dancing With Angels 1*.

During that encounter with the Holy Spirit, He instructed me and taught me many things. It was also during that magical morning that the Spirit of God told me that He was going to arrange for me to travel into the wilderness of Newfoundland and be sequestered in hiddenness with Him for a season. Again, this was a stretching of my mindset and my comfort zone. Nonetheless, the Holy Spirit informed me that He had prepared a place for us and that we would spend time together in a cabin in the mountains on that trip (see John 14:2-3).

I want to elaborate on this series of events, as it has a direct bearing on angels and opening the heavens over your life. The morning that the Lord spoke these things into my heart, I was open to hearing them, because I honestly did not believe that there was any possible way for these instructions to come to pass. The requests that the Lord made of me seemed impossible. However, as I soon began to learn, with God nothing is impossible. Perhaps the Lord will begin to speak impossible things into your heart as you read this book. These requests from the Lord required me to perform unusual acts of obedience, or what some call prophetic acts (see Matt. 19:26; Luke 18:27).

Perhaps my obedience to simply say yes to the Lord, even though I did not see any possible way for those things to come to pass, helped to open the heavens over my life. So allow me to state that obedience to the Holy Spirit is absolutely critical to opening the heavens over your life. Obedience is critical to maintaining open heavens in your sphere of influence. Amazingly and in short order, the Lord fulfilled the impossible requests that He had asked of me. The Lord had utilized angelic ministry to release financial provision and to open the door for me to travel to Africa. The trip to Africa was an extreme prophetic act of obedience on my part and was unimaginable to me at the time. My obedience to fulfill these prophetic acts played a role in transforming my life and walk with Jesus.

In obedience to the Lord's request, I extended my trip to Canada by several days. This was a real stretch for me. My flesh and carnal man earnestly desired to return to my business and "normal" life back in America. After all, I was now reduced to an impoverished state, with very little money in my pocket and no visible means of support. My rent was due, and I did not have any funds to make that payment. So the idea of staying in Canada with the Holy Spirit, though very appealing, did not make a lot of sense in the natural realm. I just could not see any possible way that I could afford to do this stuff. A trip to Africa was a preposterous idea. Even the concept of extending my Canadian adventure and seeking to find God in a cabin on a mountain somewhere seemed absurd to my carnal mind. On top of all of that, I was financially strapped and didn't even have enough money to pay for food.

However, I chose to walk in the Spirit and trust in the Lord and what I was hearing Him instruct me to do, even if it meant that I might be evicted. You could say that my flesh was warring against my spirit. You may also experience a similar struggle as you seek to open the heavens over your life. I want to elaborate on these events. I pray that this will encourage you and help the reader to understand the dynamics of opening the heavens over your life, and the role of the person of the Holy Spirit in this process.

MEETING GOD

On Sunday, December 2, 2001, I had returned to Living Waters Church in Springdale, Newfoundland, Canada. The previous day I had arranged to meet with the pastor, Dave Mercer. I shared with him about my visitation of Jesus, and how I had seen the Lord step down from the realms of Heaven into Living Waters Church on November 25, 2001. I also told Pastor Dave about the angel I had seen in his church. Dave was very cordial and encouraged me greatly. Pastor Dave listened to my testimony patiently. This was a great blessing; because of his kindness and openness to the supernatural experiences I shared with him, I was able to move ahead with some small confidence that I was not "losing it." Dave was one of the first pastors I had met who was actually anointed to pastor.

That Sunday morning, I was sort of "dancing around the sanctuary," worshiping the Lord during the praise time. As I did this, a beautiful older woman, Daisy, stopped me. She told me that the Lord had spoken to her about me. This was a shocker to me, and I stood in stunned silence waiting to hear what she would say next. She continued saying something to the effect of, "The Lord said that I was to offer to let you use my vacation cabin on the lake. For some reason the Lord wants to spend time alone with you in the wilderness. Would you like to visit my cabin?" I was once more astonished at God's goodness and His faithfulness. I remembered what the Lord had told me on Killic Island, in Botwood, just a few days before. I immediately agreed, accepting Daisy's kind offer. I knew that this was the Lord at work.

On Monday, December 3, 2001, I traveled into the mountains to find Daisy's cabin. It was small and was heated by a little wood-burning stove. Since it was extremely cold, this was a real blessing. A good friend helped me to bring in some wood, and I organized my supplies. These included a few cans of soup, some Saltine crackers, a loaf of white bread, a jar of peanut butter, some bottled water, the book *Good Morning Holy Spirit,* and my trusty King James Bible.

The instant the door closed behind my friend and they departed, the presence of the Holy Spirit fell upon me in power. The tangible presence of God enveloped me. At that precise instant, the Lord ripped open the heavens over my life. I believe that this was the fruit of my geographical obedience. Daisy's little cabin became a Mount of Transfiguration experience for me. The tangible presence of God enveloped me. Later, I would learn that what I experienced that Monday afternoon was what the Bible refers to as the glory, or *kabod*,[1] of God. I immediately began to weep as the passion and presence of Jesus flooded my spirit and the confines of the little cabin. I fell to my knees in the presence of God. There was no need to pray. There was just a knowing that I was to *be* in His presence. Just ten minutes in the real presence and glory of God will change your life forever!

After some time, I lay down on the little couch and just luxuriated in Him. The presence of the Person of the Holy Spirit seemed to penetrate every fiber of my being. This was Jesus. This was the actual presence of God. This is what He desires—just to be with us. I am not sure how long I waited in the power and presence of the Holy Spirit. I did not want to move. There was no need to think. There was a knowing that I was just to be with Him. I wept. I laughed. I smiled. I was His. He was mine.

The Lord did not speak to me. He did not make any requests. He just wanted to be with me. The Holy Spirit just wanted to have fellowship with me. I was no longer concerned about the cares of this world. The Spirit of God became my world. For a divine segment of time, I was in harmony with the Lord. There was no need to pray. There was nothing that I needed. I was at total peace, because I had Him. I was accepted by God just the way that I was. At that moment, I was still pretty much a big mess, and my life was in disarray. But that did not seem to matter to God. He loved me just the way I was, and it seemed as if I had touched Heaven for a fleeting moment of time.

It must have been several hours later that the Lord spoke to me, breaking the silence and peace that surpassed my ability to understand. The Holy Spirit said, "Are you ready now?" In hindsight, I wish that I had told the Lord that I just wanted to stay with Him and be in His presence. However, I also knew that the Lord had a plan for this special time. In my mind, I believed that the Lord wanted me to read the book *Good Morning Holy Spirit* that Margret had given me.[2] I said, "I am ready, Lord." I sat up on the couch and then moved to the small sink and splashed some cold water on my face. I could sense angels in abundance. Then I walked over to my little pack. It held my Bible and the book by Benny Hinn. I was sure that the Lord wanted me to read the book *Good Morning Holy Spirit*.

When I reached into the pack, the Lord said, "I have brought you here to teach you some things."

"Do you want me to read the book?" I asked.

Suddenly, I had a knowing that I was to read the Book of Acts instead. This was the unction of the Holy Spirit. In fact, the Holy Spirit said, "I wrote the Book of Acts and I am going to teach you from the Book of Acts." My mind began to whirl as I wondered what it meant to be taught by the Holy Spirit. At the time, this seemed to be perfectly normal to me, so I accepted the Holy Spirit's offer without hesitation. I took the Bible (the same one that had been blasted off of my chest by the heavenly ball of fire just a few nights before, as I described in my previous book. That was the night that I was transported into the heavenly realms by a strong angel and into the very presence of Jesus!), and sat down at the small table near the wood stove. It was cozy and warm.

Amazingly, when I set the Bible down, it supernaturally opened to the title page of the Book of Acts. I smiled. At that instant, I sensed that an angel had moved his hands from the pages of my Bible. He smiled at me and vanished. Every hair on my body stood on end. It appeared that this angel was working in harmony and in symphony with the plans of the Holy Spirit to minister to me. This fact gave me a real peace and a supernatural revelation about the Kingdom of God. I stared at the spot where I had just perceived the angel standing for a fleeting moment, but only the brilliant red of the Canadian sunset filtered hazily through the window there. The Holy Spirit began to speak to me in a very clear and direct manner. When the Person of the Holy Spirit began to teach me, I immediately put the angel I had sensed out of my mind. However, I was aware of the fact that there were a lot of angels in the cabin with us. In fact, it seemed that a lot of angels were also coming down from Heaven into the cabin. I could also sense that angels were going up into the heavens from the little cabin. This was, of course, all new to me. I just embraced what I was discerning during this time with the Holy Spirit.[3]

Over the course of the next two days, the Holy Spirit spoke to me and taught me—line by line and verse by verse—through the entire Book of Acts. As I would read each Scripture, the Holy Spirit would elaborate on the text. At times, He would ask me questions. At other times, I would ask Him questions, and the Lord would give me gentle and insightful answers to my questions. During this process, I began to become very comfortable with speaking to the Person of the Holy Spirit on a personal basis. I was learning to recognize His voice clearly. It seemed to be totally normal to be sitting and supernaturally speaking to the Person of the Holy Spirit. Most of the time, I spoke to Him in an audible voice. It seemed that, after a time, He also responded and dialogued with me in an audible manner. Honestly, I am not sure. However, I am sure that the Lord spoke to me clearly and precisely, teaching me various aspects and intricacies about the entire Book of Acts. The ability to hear the voice of the Holy Spirit is another fruit of an open heaven.

When I would become tired, I would ask the Lord if it was OK if I took a break. The Person of the Holy Spirit taught me late into the night during this period. I grew fatigued at times, and I would lie down and occasionally doze off. In each instance, the Lord would continue to instruct me in my dreams, and I actually dreamed about the events that were depicted in the Book of Acts. So the Lord continued to instruct me in the night season (see Job 33:15-16). I came to understand, years later, that "God dreams" are also the fruit of an open heaven. Several of those dreams were about the season that the apostle Paul was sequestered with the Lord in the desert of Arabia. Amazingly, I walked with Paul in my dreams. Paul told me how he received his revelation of Christ and the Gospel that he preached. It was not given to him by a man. He had supernatural revelation before he met the apostle Peter and James, the Lord's brother, some five years later in Jerusalem. He was given knowledge by the Person of the Holy Spirit and by the Lord Jesus Himself in the desert. Paul was taught about the Lord's Supper, or the communion table, by Christ Himself. Lord willing, I will share some of this information and revelation that I was given by the Person of the Holy Spirit in a subsequent book about the life of the apostle Paul (see Gal. 1:10-12; 1 Cor. 11:23).

SUPERNATURAL INSTRUCTION

It was the Person of the Holy Spirit who helped to teach Paul while he was in the Arabian Desert for three years. Of course, Paul did not have the Gospels for the Holy Spirit to teach him from. However, Paul did have the Torah. And the Holy Spirit taught the apostle Paul about the ministry of Christ, the Messiah, through the writings of the prophets and the Old Testament in a very similar manner that Jesus taught His disciples on the road to

Emmaus. The apostle Paul did possess personal scrolls or parchments that contained segments and books of the Old Testament teachings while he was sequestered with the Lord in the Arabian Desert. He most certainly studied these with the guidance and help of the Holy Spirit. Remember that Saul, who was transformed into Paul, was filled with the Holy Spirit shortly after his salvation (see Acts 9:17-18).

We see that kind of supernatural teaching outlined in the life of the resurrected Christ:

> *And beginning at Moses and all the Prophets, He expounded* [taught] *to them in all the Scriptures the things concerning Himself. Then they drew near to the village where they were going, and He indicated that He would have gone farther. But they constrained Him, saying, "Abide with us, for it is toward evening, and the day is far spent." And He went in to stay with them. Now it came to pass, as He sat at the table with them, that He took bread, blessed and broke it, and gave it to them. Then their eyes were opened and they knew Him; and He vanished from their sight. And they said to one another, "Did not our heart burn within us while He talked with us on the road, and while He opened the Scriptures to us?"*
> (Luke 24:27-32)

This is another example of the open heaven that was upon Jesus impacting other ordinary people in the immediate area.

This is the nature of our God. When we draw close to God, He will always draw close to us. This happened to Paul, it happened to Jesus, it happened to Cleopas on the road to Emmaus, and in some very small way, it happened to me at Daisy's little cabin in the wilderness. The Person of the Holy Spirit visited me. He taught me and instructed me about the events depicted in the Book of Acts. Those supernatural happenings, as written by the apostle Luke, became alive within my spirit. The ascension, the angels, the resurrections, the manifestations of the Holy Spirit, the Pentecosts (plural), the miracles, the persecutions, the prayer meetings, the prophetic decrees, the extravagant giving, the brotherhood of the believers, the expansion of the ministry, the martyrs, the evangelism, the translations, the demonstrations of God's power, the unbelievable conversion of Saul, Saul's transformation, the signs and wonders, the angelic ministry and the Macedonian calls, the visions, the acts of prophetic obedience to God, the growing pains of the Church, the angelic interventions, the missions trips, the discipleship of young men, the signs and wonders in prison, the visitations of Jesus, the visitations of angels, the visitations of the Holy Spirit, the riots and violence sparked by the opposition to the Gospel, the grace and favor of God, the calls to the nations, the deceptions and plots, the standing before kings and leaders, the trials, the shipwrecks, the perils, the cost to serve Christ with truth and an uncompromising spirit, the power of the Holy Spirit to protect us from harm, the pouring out of our lives as a drink offering to honor our King—it all became very real to me.

I understood that we are still writing the Book of Acts. We are still living the Book of Acts. Jesus is alive, and He has truly given us power! The events of the Book of Acts took on life in my spirit, in my world, and in my sphere of influence. They are real, and those same kinds of supernatural experiences are still available to you and me today. It is not a history book, as some intellectuals propagate. The Book of Acts was no longer a *logos* or written word to me. The Book of Acts became a living word in my heart and in my spirit; it became a *rhema* word. The Book of Acts is still unfolding today. We can still live it, we can still experience it, and we can still walk in the same kinds of signs and wonders depicted by Luke in the Book of Acts.

That was the fruit of the ministry of the Holy Spirit to me in the wilderness of Newfoundland. The Holy Spirit opened the heavens over my life. He opened up the reality of Christ's Kingdom within my heart. He birthed within me a passion and a faith for the things hoped for but not yet seen. The precious Holy Spirit became a real Person to me, and when I opened my heart and invited Him to enter, He transformed my life. He did this by opening the heavens for me. The Holy Spirit opened the heavens that are within my heart or within me. Then the Holy Spirit opened the heavens over my life and sphere of influence. He did that by opening and expounding upon the Scriptures for me. God Himself did this for me. God Himself will do this for you also. Later on, I found the passage of Scripture that so eloquently describes this type of ministry of the Holy Spirit just as Christ promised:

> *But the Helper, the Holy Spirit, whom the Father will send in My name, He will teach you all things, and bring to your remembrance all things that I said to you* (John 14:26).

After about 60 or so hours of walking through the Book of Acts with the Holy Spirit, the Lord finally said, "Do you have any other questions?"

At that moment, I was in a state of shock. I guess you could say that I was blown away by the Spirit of God. I was reeling as I sought to process the enormity of the massive amount of information and revelation that had been poured out upon me during that supernatural and enchanting time. So I said, "No, Lord."

When I did, the presence of the Holy Spirit lifted to a great degree, and the Lord said, "Now you can read my friend's book." I decided to get some fresh air first, and I stepped out once more into the cool of the day.

I took a long walk in the evening as the sun began to set over the lake nearby. The blood-red Canadian sunset turned the frozen lake into God's own personal canvas. The colors that reflected from it, at that moment, were fantastic and spectacular to imbibe with my eyes. As I breathed in the fresh, crisp, clean air, it felt as if I had also been made fresh and clean. Again, it seemed as if the Holy Spirit was walking beside me. I looked, on more than one occasion, for footprints in the snow, but found none. As the crisp winter winds whipped off the frozen, snow-covered lake, it seemed that the peaceful winds carried the gentle voices of angels singing in some unknown tongue. As I walked from time to time, I caught glimpses of the angels that seemed to be dancing around me as I promenaded in the cool of the evening. This fact no longer surprised me. Rather, it brought a smile to my face and a peace into my spirit. I understood that angels were always nearby, and that they are my friends and fellow servants of the Messiah.

Later, I returned to Daisy's little cabin and stoked the fire. Then I settled onto the little couch and began to read the book *Good Morning Holy Spirit*. I read it in less than 24 hours, and I was astonished to discover that Benny Hinn had a very similar experience with the Person of the Holy Spirit. In fact, the Holy Spirit had also taught him from the Book of Acts in a similar fashion as I had just experienced. This revelation both stunned me and delighted me simultaneously. The Father, in His wisdom, had sent

along with me, into the wilderness of Newfoundland, the very con-
firmation of the supernatural experiences I was to walk through.
Needless to say, those few days alone with the Person of the Holy
Spirit in the presence of God had a profound effect upon my life
by opening the heavens within me.

When I returned to the United States, I would often lay upon
my bed and meditate late into the night about the things I experienced in Daisy's little cabin. Over the years, I have written and
pondered these events in my heart over and over again. I have
sought the Lord for more revelation, and He has been faithful to
give it to me. During my seasons of prayer and fasting concerning
these things, I have come to many conclusions about these supernatural events. I have come to understand that one of the ministries of the Holy Spirit is to *make Heaven real* to people. The Holy
Spirit is assigned to make the Person of Christ Jesus real to people.
He is responsible for revealing and establishing Christ's Kingdom
on earth. The Holy Spirit is the Agent of *true revival* upon the
earth today (see John 14:26-28).

An important mission and ministry of the Holy Spirit is to
open the heavens over a person's life. That is the dynamic that I
experienced while I was in Newfoundland. This ministry of the
Holy Spirit was illustrated by the experience that I have just shared
about my time in Daisy's little cabin. As the presence of the Holy
Spirit begins to abide upon a person, it has the benefit of simultaneously opening the heavens over his or her life.

When the heavens open over our lives, it is easy for Christ's
Kingdom to come and for us to fulfill the mandate of Matthew
6:10: *"Your kingdom come. Your will be done on earth as it is in
Heaven."* The reason for this is that we carry God's Kingdom
within us and over us in the supernatural form of an open heaven.

When the heavens open within our heart and over someone's life, there is always a remarkable and dramatic increase in the amount of angelic activity in his or her life and sphere of influence. Remember that one of Jesus Christ's primary objectives and missions on earth was to rend open the heavens over humankind. So, one important way to increase your ability to see angels is to rend the heavens over your life. We will continue to share several easy ways that can help you to achieve this in the subsequent chapters. Let's continue to explore this dynamic of rending open the heavens in the next chapter.

ENDNOTES

1. Strong's Concordance Reference: **H3519,** kâbôd; From H3513; properly *weight*; but only figuratively in a good sense, *splendor* or *copiousness:* glorious (-ly), glory, honour (-able).

2. See *Dancing With Angels 1: How to Work With the Angels in Your Life*, Chapter 4, "Prophesying About Angels."

3. A few months later, I also experienced a very dramatic and tangible angelic visitation of this kind involving open heavens and angelic activity. This experience is illustrated in great detail in *Dancing With Angels 1,* Chapter 6, "Angels and the Lamb of God."

Chapter 5

OPENING UP THE HEAVENS OVER YOUR LIFE

In this chapter, I want to continue to build on the foundation that I laid in my previous book. I pray that this will help to stoke a renewed fire and passion for Jesus as you read my life experiences with angels. The detailed illustrations of my experiences can help you to have a better understanding of how to actually proceed and begin to pursue these same kinds of supernatural experiences with the Lord and understand how to co-labor with God's angels.

Therefore, I want to revisit a few of the initial angelic visitations that I experienced. My goal here is to give the reader practical insights into my mindset and the simple actions I took that initiated the angelic visitations in my life, which activated my ability to see angels. This will help you further understand the simplicity of walking under an open heaven and the process of activating your eyes to see. Of course, it was these initial angelic encounters that transformed my life.

Elaborating upon the concept of an open heaven and study-ing how this manifestation of Christ's Kingdom accelerates the appearance of angels and angelic activity will give us understand-ing. Again, anytime you find an open heaven, you will often find increased supernatural activity and often angelic action. As we have learned, God's angels will often carry an anointing into a geo-graphical location when they break into our environment from the realms of Heaven. These anointings can vary from angel to angel.

MANIFESTATION

I would like to recount a few modern testimonies that relate to these kinds of manifestations of angels and how they touch our five carnal or cognitive senses and also our spiritual senses. Sometimes angels stir our spirit, or what I call our "spiritual senses." Some people call this discernment. At other times we can just have a "knowing" that angels are present. At these times, it is a good idea to entertain the angels, as suggested in Hebrews 13:2, and not to quickly dismiss what we are discerning with our spiritual senses (see Eph. 1:17-18). This passage of Scripture refers to what I call our "spiritual senses," but really it refers to the ability to discern spiritual things according to the gift of discernment (see 1 Cor. 12:10). The gift of discernment at times works in conjunction with the gift of prophecy, the word of knowledge, the word of wisdom, and in harmony and symphony with the Holy Spirit. When this occurs, an individual is able to discern or see into the realm of the spirit and angels. It is important to embrace or to entertain these faint impressions.[1]

In the latter part of 2001 and through the spring, summer, and fall of 2002, I began to earnestly seek the face of Jesus. I was instantly delivered from the addiction that had so crippled my life, and after that I had a truly thankful, humbled heart. Christ had begun the process of transforming my life. So I began an intense search for the *real* Jesus. I wanted to know the Jesus of the Bible and not the Jesus "of man." I somehow understood that there was a huge difference.

I was renting a tiny house at 121 Beech Street in Bluefield, West Virginia. This was a place where I began to grow even more desperate and hungry for the real Jesus. In the process of seeking His face, I inadvertently began to have supernatural experiences. I was not aware that the testimonies from the Bible were not supposed to be experienced by new Christians. Therefore, when I read about Ezekiel and John in the Book of Revelation, I just thought those sorts of supernatural experiences, visions, and heavenly encounters were supposed to be normal for people. As far as I was concerned, the Bible said it and that settled it. In my mind, I just believed that I could have the same kind of experiences. I also thank God for the teaching ministry of Dad Kenneth E. Hagin, as his teachings helped me to understand the supernatural experiences that I was having during this season.

So, I began to lock myself in the little house and fast and pray. Actually, the Holy Spirit told me to "read, rest, fast, and pray." I would read the Gospels, look at the experiences of the people in the Bible, and rest. When I would get sleepy from reading the Word, I would just allow myself to drift off to sleep. Many of those times, as I slept, the Lord would give me vivid visions and fantastic dreams, like when I dreamed of speaking to the apostle Paul while I was in Newfoundland. These kinds of supernatural dreams increase substantially when you live under an open heaven. All the while I would be fasting. When the Lord would lead me, I would work my way through intercessory prayer. At that time, I did not know what intercession was, but I would pray in the way that the Holy Spirit would direct me.

I prayed for forgiveness and cleansing. I prayed for faces of people I did not know. I prayed for unborn children. I prayed for God to stop abortion. I prayed for the president. I prayed for the peace of Israel. I prayed for everything that I could think of to pray for, and then I would pray for the things that I saw and felt that the Lord wanted me to pray for. After a point, I would come to a place where there was nothing else to pray for, and I would begin to pray in the Spirit for hours on end. Then, when I was released from praying this way, I would ask the Lord what He wanted me to do at that point. Usually, He would instruct me to wait on His presence.

It was during this time that I discovered Psalm 27:14: *"Wait on the LORD; be of good courage, and He shall strengthen your heart; wait, I say, on the LORD!"* Psalm 46:10 also gives us a scriptural basis for this kind of prayer: *"Be still, and know that I am God...."* Some people call this "meditative prayer." However, I was just seeking the Lord and trying to be obedient to the Holy Spirit as I had begun to hear His voice very clearly after my trip to Newfoundland, Canada, in 2001. I just relaxed, luxuriated, and waited in His presence, like I had done in Daisy's cabin. In this way, I pressed violently into Christ's Kingdom without ceasing for days on end.

So I would just wait on God. Sometimes I would just wait for days. I would read, rest, fast, and pray, asking the Lord to reveal Himself to me. I wanted to know Him as a friend. I had read the Scripture that told me that God would stay closer to me than a brother. So I began to ask Him for that kind of friendship and closeness (see Prov. 18:24). It did not take too long before the Lord began to answer me and reveal Himself as the King of kings. Soon, Jesus began to reveal other aspects of His Kingdom to me. Eventually, supernatural things started to transpire in that little house. I began to hear laughter, and there would be noises in the kitchen. At first, I was a little concerned. However, since the presence and glory of the Lord was thick and heavy in my little tabernacle of meeting, I had a supernatural kind of peace about these mystical events that were unfolding around me! Then I realized that I was hearing angels, so I decided to embrace what was happening and to entertain them.

I had read the book of Hebrews and it suggested that some people can "entertain" angels without being aware of them. So in my mind, I reasoned that if people could entertain God's angels without knowing about it, then it would be possible for me to entertain the angels that were visiting me on purpose! I would welcome the angels into my little house. I would actually speak to them. Kathy and I still entertain angels in Moravian Falls this way. The angels like it! I would speak to the angels, saying, "Make yourselves comfortable. Help yourselves to some Kool Aid and ramen noodles." At that time, it was pretty much all I had in the pantry, so this was an added motivation to fast and pray.

One evening the activity was especially intense. I was certain that there were angels laughing and frolicking on the couch in the small living room. I just had a *knowing* that angels were in the house. Later, I began to realize that this knowing was actually the unction of the Holy Spirit (see 1 John 2:20). So I got up from the floor of my prayer closet where I had been waiting upon the Lord. This prayer closet was the six-foot by four-foot micro bathroom. I decided to go into the living room and see for myself what was actually happening. I had been hearing things moving and a lot of what sounded like laughter. I could have sworn that I was hearing people whispering in a foreign language. When I turned the corner, I was astonished to see a large angel with his large wings outstretched. He was laughing and seemed to be joking with several other angels in the room. He was waving his wings back and forth over the other angels. He was smiling and laughing! They were having a really good romp session.

When I saw him and he saw me, all the angels stopped for a second and there was a pregnant pause and silence. I looked carefully at the large angel. I realized that this was the same angel I had seen in the heavens with Jesus. As a matter of fact, this was one of the four angels that the Lord had told me that He was "appointing" to me. I knew this angel, and it appeared that he was about eight feet tall, but it was hard to be sure, as he was sort of hunched over in the tiny room. I also looked at the other angels in the room. There were about six or seven angels there, and they appeared to be adolescent men. A stunned silence hung in the room for an uncomfortable moment. The other angels were all much smaller, and they seemed to be as surprised to see me as I was to see them. They were all clad in immaculate white garments, and they all possessed a pair of brilliant white wings. I was astonished, to say the least. However, I think that my presence surprised or even startled them even more than they did me!

They looked around at one another and then looked at the big angel. He seemed to be the one in charge of the group. Then they all looked at me and began to laugh again. I was stunned! I blinked my eyes a few times as if they were malfunctioning. When I opened them, I could no longer see my visitors, but I could still hear them laughing. So I just threw up my hands and told them that they were welcome, and to stay just as long as they wanted to. So that is how I first began to entertain open heavens and the Lord's angels. Perhaps this testimony will encourage you and help you to entertain angels too.

From that night on, I could always sense the angels in and around 121 Beech Street. At times I would see the big winged fellow with my eyes open, and he would always give me a reassuring smile. He has blond hair and really perfect teeth. This particular angel is assigned to release provision and protection to me in my sphere of influence. So you could accurately say that he is my guardian angel. This is one of the angels that seems to follow me around the earth. His wings are unbelievably clean and seem to have a phosphorescent glow about them. After that night, when I would come into the house at Beech Street after working, the power and anointing of the Lord would be very heavy at times. Sometimes I would walk through the old black front door and I would just fall out under the power of the Spirit onto the floor. Then I would often be taken out into "visions of God." Again, visions are another supernatural fruit of living under an open heaven.

Some folks call these "third heaven" experiences. One day I put the key in the front door, and when I stepped across the threshold, I just fell out. I did not even have the chance to close the front door. It was not until about 10:30 or 11:00 that night that I "came back into my body." It is possible that I somehow "dug a well" or opened a path into the realms of Heaven while I lived and worshiped the Lord at 121 Beech Street. Perhaps an open heaven had ripped open over the little house and my life through my intense prayers and fasting. One day, with the grace of God, I will ask the Lord more about these things. I do know that Ezekiel also had similar experiences. Later in 2004, I began to believe that I had somehow been blessed to unlock an open heaven in or over that little house (see Rev. 4:1; Deut. 28:12; Matt. 3:15; John 1:51; Luke 3:21). It is possible that the fragrance of Heaven sort of clung to me, and I carried an open heaven with me as I began to travel into the nations. I believe that you can do that. The open heavens upon an individual can actually impact and rend the heavens of other regions and nations that are within a person's calling or sphere of influence. We will look at this dynamic of carrying an open heaven to other regions in more detail in the subsequent chapters. This will illustrate how open heavens often work in harmony with the Holy Spirit and angelic ministry to further and manifest Christ's Kingdom for His glory alone.

At times I would, indeed, see the large angel that seemed to take up residence on the old, worn-out couch in the tiny living room at 121 Beech Street. As I matter of fact, I was reluctant to move from the little house when the Lord instructed me to do so because of the intensity of the spiritual activity that occurred there. I am convinced that the Lord will reward your efforts to rip open the heavens over your life too. I believe that opening the heavens over a region or even a nation is still quite possible today.

The Lord will begin to use ordinary people to work with His angels to open the heavens in certain regions in the coming days. This was the spark that set the Argentinean Revival in motion in the mid-1940s. These kind of open heavens and angelic activities will also repeat in the coming season to release global outpourings throughout the earth.[2] In the next chapter, I want to share more details about opening the heavens over a region working with the unction of the Holy Spirit and angelic help

ENDNOTES

1. For more details see *Dancing With Angels 1*, Chapter 14, "Angels and the Gift of Discerning of Spirits."

2. See *Dancing With Angels 1*, Epilogue for more details on this.

Chapter 6

OPENING THE HEAVENS OVER REGIONS WITH ANGELIC HELP

In Acts 1:8-11, we are given a glimpse into the last moments of Christ's resurrected life on earth before He ascends back into Heaven to sit at the right hand of our Father. We see that Jesus departs or ascends through an open heaven back into the arms of His Father. This is a parabolic picture of Christ's mission to open the heavens over all of humankind. Just like Christ, we can ascend through an open heaven to return into the arms of our heavenly Father, too.

The last words that Jesus spoke on that day are very important. After He promised us the gift of the baptism of the Holy Spirit, Christ gave you and me these instructions:

> *You shall receive power when the Holy Spirit has come upon you; and you shall be witnesses to Me in Jerusalem, and in all Judea and Samaria, and to the end of the earth (Acts 1:8).*

I want to dissect this statement for the sake of clarity. Jesus was drawing a map for believers to use when proclaiming and demonstrating His Kingdom on Earth.

EXPANDING ANOINTING

First, the Lord tells the people to witness about Him in Jerusalem (their hometown), then to witness about Him in all Judea (that is a region surrounding the area of the city of Jerusalem), then to witness about Him in Samaria (that is a territory that was 42 miles north of Jerusalem), and finally to the end of the earth. This is a principle and spiritual dynamic that is always found in Christ's Kingdom. The Lord will anoint a person to witness or preach about the Cross in his own city first. Remember that we have seen, from Christ's own example, that He began His ministry in His own hometown of Nazareth. Jesus started off by preaching in His own church (or synagogue). Then, the Lord will add an additional anointing to expand a person's call to a region. He will then give additional anointing to allow a person to minister in a territory. And finally, the Lord will increase the anointing upon an individual to witness or preach about the Cross to the ends of the earth (other nations).

It is also important for us to realize that the Holy Spirit comes upon us to enable us to fulfill this mandate. However, we need to understand that there are many different levels of the Holy Spirit and the anointing of the Holy Spirit. The Holy Spirit gives spiritual gifts to people. However, there is a difference between operating in a spiritual gift and having the power or anointing of the Holy Spirit come upon you. The anointing of the Holy Spirit can come upon a person for a few moments for a ministry purpose. The anointing of the Holy Spirit can also come upon a person and abide with him or her in a continual way. That should be our goal—not to taste the anointing occasionally, but to live in the anointing of the Holy Spirit. Living under this kind of tangible anointing of the Holy Spirit is what I call an open heaven, and this dynamic is possible for you today. You *can* live under an open heaven. You *can* live in the abiding anointing of the Holy Spirit. Christ did.

It is important to understand this dynamic. We need to grow in Christ's Kingdom, line upon line, precept upon precept. We can grow in the power of the Holy Spirit. We can also grow into the very image of Christ Jesus. I call this dynamic of the Holy Spirit's anointing and multiplication in a person's life his or her sphere of influence or sphere of anointing. You must be obedient to minister in your own city, then wait for the Lord to promote you to a region, then a territory, and finally, for God to call you out into the nations of the earth. This dynamic unfolded in this exact fashion in my life. God increases the amount of the anointing and power of the Holy Spirit in your life in increments. This process of growing in the anointing is in direct relationship to our obedience to the Lord and what He calls us to do in terms of ministry and our lives. Obedience to the Holy Spirit is critical to grow in His power and anointing. That is also why it is critical that we learn to hear the voice of the Holy Spirit clearly and learn to obey God in every aspect of our lives.

If you ask most ministers who have an international sphere of influence, you will find that this process was also evident in their lives. If a person seeks to go from his city to the nations, this will often lead to heartache and disappointment. The reason for this is that they have overstepped their sphere of influence or sphere of anointing. It is also likely that their actions are outside of God's perfect plans and will, no matter how "good" their actions appear to be. I am not saying there will be no rewards for well-meaning people like this, but it is possible that they may find themselves in the position that we see Jesus describe in Matthew 7:20-23. If the Lord has called you to be a pastor, it would be a mistake to become an evangelist. Make sure that your election and calling are sure (see 2 Peter 1:10).

Another important aspect of this progressive evolution of ministry is that it allows the Lord to open the heavens over your life to the exact degree that you need for your specific calling. I will share how the sphere of influence or sphere of anointing upon my life gradually increased. I began to see the heavens open up over my life in my city, various regions, territories, and ultimately nations in which I have been Christ's witness. It is important that you understand this dynamic or spiritual principle if you are seeking to be used by the Lord in the ministry. Sometimes people who are highly anointed and called by God miss their true calling and do not walk in the Lord's perfect will for their lives and ministries. Some people unwittingly miss God's perfect will. They thereby miss achieving the most important things that God has ordained for them to accomplish through their lives and God-ordained ministries (see Rom. 12:2).

We need to live out of God's perfect will for our lives and not our own carnal agendas. Some people minister out of their own strength without considering God's will at all. Some people step out prematurely into the nations without God's anointing and protection. Others are disobedient by not moving to the next level or sphere of influence to which the Lord has called them. This kind of disobedience will quench the anointing of the Holy Spirit and clutter up or even close the open heavens over their lives. For example, some people live their lives in obedience in one area, like their finances, but go their own way in others. We should seek to live in a lifestyle of perfect obedience to the Lord.

Back to Acts 1 for a moment, look at these verses:

> *Now when He* [Jesus] *had spoken these things, while they watched, He was taken up, and a cloud received Him out of their sight. And while they looked steadfastly toward heaven as He went up, behold, two men* [Christ's angels] *stood by them in white apparel* (Acts 1:9-10).

Here we see the Lord's angels prophesying to us about open heavens. In fact, what we really see in this passage of Scripture is the description of the open heaven that surrounded Jesus and the subsequent angelic encounter. Not only do the people here, *"the men of Galilee,"* have an angelic visitation under the open heaven, but the angels also speak to them, prophesying:

> *Men of Galilee, why do you stand gazing up into heaven? This same Jesus, who was taken up from you into heaven, will so come in like manner as you saw Him go into heaven* (Acts 1:11).

In defense of the men of Galilee who witnessed this open heaven angelic encounter, at times when the heavens open up and you begin to see and hear into the spirit, you will frequently find yourself standing by with a dazed look on your face and your mouth hanging agape! This is an additional example of how Peter, James, and John were impacted by the open heaven that was over Jesus. Again, the disciples entered into the spirit by being in proximity to the open heaven that was upon Christ.

When the heavens open over your life, it is very possible that you will see the Lord come in a like manner, and it is also possible that you will encounter angelic activities in and around your life. Let's look at some early angelic activities that seemed to manifest in my life as the heavens were opened. My sphere of influence was increased from my city to regions, then territories, and eventually the nations. You can follow this same pattern that the Lord has outlined too. God is ready, willing, and able to open the heavens over your life and transform who you are in Christ. Finally, I believe that open heavens are critical to achieving God's calling upon your life. So again, it is crucial to rip or rend open the heavens over your life. One of the benefits of an open heaven over your life is the anointing or gifting to see and interact with angels and co-labor with them to impact the realms of earth. Getting the heavens opened is not always a super-spiritual affair. The whole thing can hinge upon obedience and repentance.

These next few testimonies will help us to understand how open heavens and angels can manifest their presence to all of our carnal and spiritual senses. Sometimes, the ability to see angels can be activated by carefully paying attention to slight leadings and urges stirred up within our spirits by the Holy Spirit. Often it is easy to overlook these leadings, so we must begin to exercise our ability to discern even the slightest nudge or whisper of the precious Holy Spirit. Recognizing and working in harmony with the Holy Spirit only comes by investing time with Him. This gift and skill also takes patience and practice to develop. I like to encourage folks to practice persistence, keep on knocking, and keep on asking God for His Kingdom. Getting the heavens opened over your life or a specific geographic region can be a process. At times, you will need to practice patience and persistence as you are led by the Holy Spirit to perform acts of obedience and occasionally, sacrifice (see Heb. 5:14; Luke 18:3-5).

ANGELS AND OPEN HEAVENS IN SOUTHWEST VIRGINIA

During the King of Glory Music Festival in 2002, I met Steve and Becky Asbury. They were attending the festival and were deeply touched when they saw a woman's deaf ear open. Steve received a miraculous healing when a large, painful tumor disappeared from his lower back during this time. Steve also experienced an unusual encounter with an angel when he visited me at 121 Beech Street in 2002. At this time, my sphere of influence was still mostly confined to my home town and to Infirmity Prayer Service, a small church in the city. I had been faithful to reach out to the lost in my city as I had been directed by the Lord. I did this through the King of Glory Music Festival for four consecutive years. Many people began to recognize that the heavens were opened as this outreach progressed over the years.[1] So, again, this unfolding of my sphere of influence and open heavens over my life had a very humble beginning. The heavens were rent by repentance and obedience.

Steve came to visit and to fellowship with me. We were going to go and grab a bite to eat. I had been praying earlier and had seen the big angel sitting on the old couch in his usual spot at 121 Beech Street. When Steve walked into the house, he immediately said that he smelled "fresh-baked bread." I laughed and told him to grab a seat while I finished getting ready to go, and I stepped into the bathroom. In a few seconds, I heard a loud thud. I walked back into the little living room to see Steve prostrate on the floor. In a flash, I realized what had happened. Steve had sat on the big angel!

I let him lay there for a minute and then thought that I should get him up. I said, "Hey buddy, what happened to you?"

Steve said, "I don't know, but when I sat down on the couch, it felt like I got hit by a lightning bolt, and I passed out!" I told him not to worry, it was only an angel! Steve cocked his head a little to the right and said, "Yeah, right." We went on out, and I did not try to convince him that he had an encounter with an angel, but Steve soon began to realize that he was experiencing angelic activities.

I have often heard it said that the anointing is "better caught than taught." I think that it is also true for the ability or the gifting to see into the realms of the spirit and to discern angels. It is possible that Steve Asbury caught something over the course of the next few years of our friendship. Here is a testimony that I penned on the night that we witnessed the heavens open over southwest Virginia, followed by one of Steve's testimonies from the third King of Glory Music Festival held in 2003.

OPEN HEAVENS AND ANGELS IN THE PARK, AUGUST 2003

Tonight my friend, Steve Asbury, and I went to the Sara Creasy Amphitheatre where the King of Glory Music Festival was going to be held. We were praying and seeking the face of the Lord for direction and guidance for the ministry that will happen at the meeting. We also prayed for the Lord to send His angels to release cleansing and protection over the shelter and region. When we arrived at the park, the sky was totally overcast. It had been raining on and off. The sky was covered with heavy black clouds over the amphitheater, and we could not see the sky or moon. There was just a dull glow behind the ominous, dark grey cloud covering.

We stepped up onto the platform and began to pray and decree Scriptures into the night. It was about 8:47 P.M. I was praying and decreeing Psalm 24 and Revelation 4. We were asking the Lord to open the heavens over the region. Suddenly, the anointing of the Holy Spirit began to manifest, and the tangible presence of the Lord began to fall. In less than about 120 seconds (this is no exaggeration), a portion of the skies became bright and crystal clear. The overcast sky turned a bright evening blue within a perfectly formed circle above the grounds of the amphitheater. This supernatural circle was about half a mile in radius. In the opening, we could see the half-moon shining brightly, and the stars began to twinkle in the open heavens above.[3]

The supernatural circle in the park was truly a miraculous display of God's power and a sign and wonder in the sky! I have only witnessed a phenomenon like this two times before. Once was last year in a prophetic experience in this same location. The other time was in Uganda when a beautiful double rainbow appeared behind the platform at a crusade in the city of Jinja. That night there were hundreds of miracles and healings. The perfect circle that we witnessed tonight was truly awesome.

Even more spectacular was the perceptible presence of God. The anointing was as thick as a milkshake and tangible! I mean, it was physically there; you could actually see the glory of God settle in the park in front of the stage and grounds! It looked like a beautiful, perceptible purple fog. It seemed that you could actually taste it! You could see God's manifest glory. A cloud sort of hovered over the infield. I was sensing that there were a lot of angels that were coming down through the perfect circle that had formed in the overcast night sky.

We continued to pray and to prophesy into the open heavens. I began to decree for John 1:51 to be released in this place, asking the Lord to release legions of warring angels into southwest Virginia to perform His word and execute His will. In a moment or two, the atmosphere became electric, and I could almost feel and see the angels that were invading the park. I believe that they were dancing in a circle in the front of the platform. I am not positive, but that is what I was sensing. It was powerful. Steve and I were getting touched mightily by the Holy Spirit. So we started to meander around the area where I sensed the angels were dancing in the circle and were calling out to God for more of His glory to fall!

As we began to meander around the concrete slab in front of the stage, we began to get detailed words of knowledge for healing. We received numbers of these and wrote them down and planned to call them out at the festival when the Lord directed us to. The anointing continued to build, and I started to feel a familiar presence of my angelic friend. This is the angel that shows up and helps to release the gift of healings. Electricity began to build in my left arm and hand. It seemed that the electricity was actually sizzling in the evening air and the purple glory cloud of the Lord. The manifest presence of the Holy Spirit was electric!

The healing angel had drawn close, and I could actually smell him. I know this angel. He is a healing angel. Of course! This was the same angel that was with me when the cancer patient was healed in Lawrence, Kansas. That was the time that Jesus healed a woman's numb and limp left arm. This was the same angel that was in Kansas City the night that a young girl's spine straightened out and her withered hand was loosed and her left thumb grew half an inch. This is the same angel that was in Pasadena when Lori Seidensticker had a portion of her amputated toes grow back. I realized that this was the same healing angel that was in Toronto when Gerta Menkie's deaf left ear was opened.

This is the same angel that was in Las Vegas when a woman's left leg grew two inches and she could walk normally for the first time in 51 years, and the blind intercessor was healed! This was the same angel that had stood behind me in Lilongwe, Malawi, when the Holy Spirit told me that He was going to open blind eyes as a prophetic sign. This was the same angel that had stood behind me and whispered into my left ear as I prayed for Leonard, the man who grew an eyeball. This was the same angel that had worked with the team as we saw 21 totally blind people healed under a tree in a refugee camp. We also saw 24 others have their partial blindness and cataracts instantly healed. We watched their cataracts dissolve in front of our eyes. All that happened in about 30 minutes as the healing angel stood by. Now, this same healing angel was here in Bluefield, Virginia! Thank You, Jesus, for You are no respecter of persons! Wow!

I could taste the honey! I could feel the electricity of the healing anointing coursing up and down my back and into my hands. I understood the mantle had fallen and the heavens had opened! Steve accidentally bumped into the angel and began to "tingle all over," and he cried out, "I can taste Pop-Tarts in my mouth!" His hands were also burning, and there was truly a corporate anointing for healing released into this place. It is the anointing that this healing angel brings when he comes. The Kingdom of Heaven had invaded earth.

Steve started to just walk repeatedly into the spot where the angel was standing. He just wanted to feel the glory that the angel was releasing. So Steve walked through the "glory zone" about 20 times. I had a few passes through the spot, too. Each time, I would smell the fragrance of frankincense, and the fire and electricity on my body would seem to increase. Finally, Steve fell out on the grass and lay in the pool of glory and soaked in the wet grass and the glory of God. We stayed in the presence of the Lord like this for about an hour. We got totally "smashed" or drunk in the Spirit as we prayed and continued to call down legions of the Lord's angelic hosts to minister in the region. We called upon the Lord to release legions of angelic warriors to transform the region for God's glory. During this whole time, we were laughing and luxuriating in the tangible purple glory and presence of the Holy Spirit. It seemed that when the Holy Spirit descended, the heavens opened and a bunch of angels just showed up! We continued to commune with the Lord, reveling in the

Holy Spirit and loving on Jesus. For a time it seemed as if we had touched Heaven on earth with all the angels and glory that was around us in the park.

STEVE ASBURY'S TESTIMONY, AUGUST 2003

Kevin and I were praying at the amphitheater in the park in Bluefield, Virginia, a few nights before the King of Glory Music Festival of 2003. It was just the two of us. We were praying for God's presence to show up for the festival Saturday. We prophesied many things over the area and into the winds, at one point almost yelling into the air. As we were doing this, the sky turned very dark, and the only light place was a real big circle in the clouds right above us. Light was shining down through the open circle in the clouds above us. We began to feel the presence of the Lord strongly after that. I was walking beside Kevin as we walked around the amphitheater and grounds. Suddenly, it felt like we walked through something. It felt like an angelic presence; I wasn't quite sure. As I walked through it, I began to taste sweet tarts or something like honey in my mouth.

The presence of God was so strong that I stumbled on the spot. I turned to Kevin and told him to walk through the spot as well. He walked through it and stumbled as well. We were both pretty freaked out, but we both kept walking back and forth across the spot. Each time we walked through the spot, we felt the presence of God getting a little stronger. Finally, I became overwhelmed by an unexplained feeling of just wanting to stay on that spot. So we walked through the spot one more time, and then we both fell to the ground there, and just became like supernaturally glued to the ground! We stayed that way (glued to the ground on the spot) for about another 45 minutes or so. Neither of us wanted to get up because of the feeling that lying on the spot gave us. It is hard to describe how it felt. I guess that an unexplained peace and electricity would be one way to describe it. When we left, I tasted sweet tarts or honey all the way home (see Ps. 34:8; Rev. 10:10; Ezek. 3:3).

During the King of Glory Festival in 2003, the Lord did in fact do many wonderful things, and there were many testimonies of miracles and healings. I am certain that the angelic activity and the healing angel that we encountered 72 hours prior to the festival played an important part in those supernatural events. I am also sure that the open heaven that we saw ripped open accomplished something in the heavenly realms over that region. I believe there is still free access in that place even today. Let's look at a short testimony from someone who was in attendance at the King of Glory Festival in 2003. This will validate these last testimonies and also help to reveal the benefits, or fruit, of an open heaven.

CHUCK LOOSLI'S TESTIMONY ABOUT THE KING OF GLORY FESTIVAL, SEPTEMBER 2003

I just returned from the King of Glory 2003 festival in West Virginia. It was an amazing time, very much like Las Vegas. At least 12 persons gave their lives to Jesus, and as many as 400 rededicated themselves to Him. One woman's leg grew, tumors on the ovaries of one woman were dissolved, deaf ears were opened, and there were those who had their eyesight healed. A woman was taken off of a ventilator and was able to return home from the hospital. Other healings were also seen during this time.

The Holy Spirit came down in a great way, touching all of those present. There was a great healing and unifying work done amongst the local presbytery. Racial and denominational barriers were torn down as well. Many had new experiences with Holy Spirit as He came down upon a "Fire Tunnel" formed by those who had come from the United States, Canada, and England. Truly, there was an open heaven over that place. One local pastor had to be carried home and put in his bed! The next day, he was still very much "drunk in the Spirit" and walked through his church laying hands on his parishioners, causing them to fall under the power of the Holy Spirit.

I believe that Virginia and West Virginia have been eternally changed through this awesome demonstration of the love of Jesus Christ. All glory belongs to the Lord, of course, but isn't it wonderful how He has chosen to use people to do His work?

As I have stated in the past, there is a strong correlation among open heavens, the anointing of the Holy Spirit, and angelic activity. The Holy Spirit is certainly responsible for releasing the gifts of the Spirit. The anointing of the Holy Spirit is responsible for much of what people call the power gifts. The anointing is critical. The power gifts could be considered the gift of healing, the gift of miracles, the gift of the word of knowledge, the gift of the word of wisdom, and the gift of prophecy. I believe that at times open heavens are critical to releasing these manifestations of the Kingdom of God. At times, the open heavens over an individual and the anointing of the Holy Spirit will release these power gifts of the Spirit. We need to be in constant touch with the precious Holy Spirit at all times.

At other times angels will be loosed by the Lord to work in symphony and harmony with the Holy Spirit and His gifts. However, angels can at times co-labor with an individual to manifest Christ's Kingdom and the gifts of the Spirit. I am in no way seeking to minimize the absolute significance and importance of the Holy Spirit. On the contrary, I am seeking to acknowledge the Holy Spirit, the anointing of the Holy Spirit, and the gifts of the Holy Spirit. What I want to make clear is that, at times, the angels of God will work in harmony, unity, and symphony with the Holy Spirit to manifest the Kingdom of Christ upon the earth. There will be times when this supernatural symphony will result in opening the heavens over an individual, a region, or even an entire nation. It is important for us to learn to understand and recognize these spiritual dynamics and manifest Christ's Kingdom as we go with the Gospel. Open heavens play an important role in this scenario too. At times, an individual can carry an open heaven with him or her from one geographic area to another region or territory. At other times, the Lord can send angels to break open the heavens in a chosen geographical location. In the subsequent chapters, we will look at several examples of how the Holy Spirit works in harmony with angelic ministry to open the heavens over geographical areas and manifest Christ's Kingdom.

By now you should understand the importance of open heavens to a person's ability to see into the spirit and perceive angels. Perhaps you are ready to press into the Kingdom and to seek to rip open the heavens over your life. Let me encourage you to invest a season in prayer and fasting at this point. Once you have been given some direction and leading by the Holy Spirit, you will be ready to begin the process of rending the heavens. In the next chapter, I will share several scriptural principles, practical examples, and tools and testimonies that can help you in this process. I pray that the Lord Himself will stir you up and give you the guidance as you read on.

ENDNOTES

1. After that assignment was complete, the Lord began to expand my area of influence and gradually opened doors for me to other cities and regions. Later, I took the King of Glory outreach to Africa and held miracle crusades in many cities there. We continue to minister with the King of Glory outreach to Africa and other nations today as the Lord leads (see 2 Cor. 2:1).

2. Chuck Loosli, a.k.a. Baked Alaska, Wasilla, Alaska.

3. This was not the first sign that was associated with the King of Glory Festivals. In 2002, the Lord gave us an exclamation point to the second festival. That sign happened when we saw a large, bright shooting star streak across the sky for an extended period of time. It was the largest and most dramatic shooting star that we had ever seen. It was like God was sealing the events of the day with a promise of more to come.

Chapter 7

More Testimonies of Angelic Encounters Under Open Heavens

In August 2002, after the King of Glory Festival, I had begun to experience an increase of angelic activity. I was beginning to recognize the relationship among angelic activity, healings, and open heavens, and the Lord began to open up my sphere of influence. I began to travel to other states to minister and loose the Kingdom of Heaven. Many times, this included the release of angelic activities. After the festival that year, I was invited by Nate Nagelkirk to come with him to Grand Rapids to minister in a few small meetings called "Fire in the Night." I had met Nate in Tanzania in 2001. It was Nate's desire to release signs and wonders in his city, and he hoped that the Lord might use me to do this. During those meetings there were, indeed, several supernatural signs, and I began to see the angels of God at work.

One evening we had a prayer meeting at the House of Prayer in Grand Rapids. Bob Cegelis was in attendance and was impacted by stirrings of the supernatural. He began to sense, discern, and step into the angelic realm. Bob's testimony is a good example of how angels can manifest to all of our senses, including the spiritual eyes of our heart. Bob was powerfully touched, and his experience had a powerful impact on his life and ministry. Here is his testimony in his own words.

BOB CEGELIS' TESTIMONY

There were several of us in the West Michigan International Prayer Center, and we were worshiping the Lord. After a while, I felt a presence enter the upper prayer room. I began to look around the room. I began to see what looked like a golden mist developing on a certain spot near the center of the room. When I looked at this spot, I could see, for lack of a better term, an aura of golden light. This amber or golden light seemed to shimmer and was in motion. It reminded me of an ornamental snow globe, but the manifestation was much larger. I could actually see golden flakes of glory shimmering in the room.

Kevin encouraged me to actually lie down on that spot. He believed that the Lord was going to release a healing to my heart. When I did lie there, the power of the Lord came upon my body. I was not able to move and felt like I was glued to the floor. There was a very hot and almost uncomfortable sensation that began to move through my heart and chest. I was certain that the Lord was actually releasing a healing into my life. Perhaps it had to do with our calling to minister to orphans and the fatherless. For some time, I had been struggling with doubt about what I felt the Lord was calling us to do.

You might say that I suffered from hope deferred as Proverbs 13:12 talks about, *"Hope deferred makes the heart sick..."* I was sure that the Lord was doing something. Soon the heat turned into the joy of the Lord and I began to laugh, and I received some kind of healing. You could say it was an inner healing or a deliverance of sorts.

I can honestly say that with my natural eyes I saw the "golden atmosphere" over a section of the prayer room. Certainly, I would ascertain that something supernatural was transpiring, and the Kingdom of Heaven had come among us that night. There was a tangible manifestation of the ministry that night. Almost immediately after this encounter, we began to get the breakthrough in the natural with our hopes and plans to minister to orphans. To that point in time, we had been in a real struggle and battle to move forward with our plans for ministry. We felt the Lord had given us the vision to minister to the orphans full time in our city of Grand Rapids, but we were not able to go forward with our ministry plans very quickly.

Today we are still working in the unfolding ministry. Even more recently, 2006, we have passed through tremendous opposition to our adoption of three young children. We now have the final decree from the courts, and we do have a renewed strength and faith that with God all things are possible and He will have His way. He is the God of the impossible. Your friends in Christ to the nations, one orphan at a time![1]

One thing that I have discovered as I have encountered and experienced open heavens is that they play a role in releasing a person into his or her God-ordained destiny and call. Perhaps you know that you have been called by God but have not been able to fully step into your calling. It is possible that if you press into the Lord and seek to rend the heavens over your life, you will find a supernatural release from the Kingdom of Heaven and begin to move into your destiny. I want to encourage you to press into God's Kingdom and seek to find a situation where you can invest time in an open heaven. These times of waiting upon the Lord, in or under an open heaven, can often be life-changing.

SEEING ANGELS

It was during this period of my life that the Lord began to open my ability to see into the realm of angels and to learn the simple ways that we can co-labor with them. These coincided with the heavens opening over my life, too. There were other people who were impacted by the angels that seemed to hang around with me in this season. Steve Asbury was one of those folks. As time passed, Steve also had the eyes of his heart opened, and he also began to see angels. In the subsequent testimony, Steve was given a parabolic vision that may help people understand the dynamics of seeing into the spiritual realm. In this experience, Steve had an "open-eyed" encounter with an angel. This experience was both refreshing and real. Perhaps Steve's experience in the open heaven in the previous chapter helped to activate the eyes of his heart to both see and hear from the realms of Heaven. Again, open heavens are very important to accelerating a person's ability to see into the spirit and obtain revelation from the Lord and His Kingdom. Here is Steve's testimony about one of the angels that he began to discern with regularity:

On my property is an artesian spring. Many people who come to visit my family are drawn to this spring for some reason. My wife and I had the chance to wash the feet of Kevin Basconi and Simon Oliver, another evangelist, in the spring. Several people have told us that they have observed angels at our spring. In the beginning, I was not too sure about these claims. For me, the spring is just a place of quiet meditation and prayer.

One evening, after work, while I was sitting on my patio, I happened to glance down at the spring. I saw a young, blond-headed angel, dressed in white, crouching on the rock in front of the spring. He was looking into the water as if staring at something. I was overwhelmed and a bit freaked out to see an angel at my house! I suddenly felt an urgency to run down to the spring. When I got to the still waters of my little pond at the spring, I did not see the angel anymore. For some reason, I felt that I was supposed to crouch in the same spot the angel was crouching and look where the angel was looking.

As I did, I saw the reflection off the clear, cold water. In the reflection I saw my house and the trees around it. I knew that I had to look deeper to see what the angel was looking at. Somehow, I thought that the angel was trying to show me something. I looked twice, and again saw the house and the trees. On the third time I looked, I saw the same thing. On the fourth time, I looked and I saw through the surface to the bottom of the spring. It was then that I received the revelation that seeing into the spirit is like looking into that spring. A brick is not a brick, wood is not wood, and dirt is not dirt. A reflection is not a reflection. We must look *through* the reflections to what is on the other side (in the spirit realm), just like the angel was trying to show me.

I challenge anyone, on a sunny day, to look into a pool of water and look past the reflection that is there. It may take a little while, but you will see the bottom through the reflection. That is how you will see past the physical and into the spiritual realm. But we must look at all things, just as we look into the water, past the reflection.[2]

Some people have had their ability to see angels activated by the Spirit of God, and at times they can see, hear, taste, touch, smell, and discern spirits. Angels are spirits (see Heb. 1:7,14). The ability to see angels is called discernment by a lot of folks. But discernment can also simply mean having a "divine knowing" that angels are present.[3] Remember that the ability to fine-tune our carnal and spiritual senses and to discern the angelic activity can be a process. At times, it is necessary to be dedicated and diligent in the pursuit of the Kingdom of Heaven.

INHERITANCE

I want to stress that you do not need to be a spiritual giant or a member of the five-fold ministry to see or experience the realm of angels. There is a theology that promotes the idea that you need to be a "chosen vessel" to have the ability to see into the realms of the Spirit. I beg to differ, as that is not God's heart. This may have well been true of those people who were under the Old Covenant or the Law of Moses. At that time, only certain folks, mostly prophets, were given the Holy Spirit—men like Moses, Joshua, Elijah, Ezekiel, King David, and others. Today, however, we are no longer under the Old Covenant, but rather a new and better covenant with Christ Jesus. Hebrews bears this out:

> *In that He [Jesus] says, "A new covenant," He has made the first obsolete. Now what is becoming obsolete and growing old is ready to vanish away* (Hebrews 8:13).

And we can see this principle clearly illustrated again:

> *For this reason He [Jesus] is the Mediator of the new covenant, by means of death, for the redemption of the transgressions under the first covenant, that those who are called may receive the promise of the eternal inheritance* (Hebrews 9:15).

We will look at this scriptural principle in greater detail later in the book. We will investigate the fact that we are all called to be royal priests after the order of Melchizedek.

One of the wonderful promises of Christ's new covenant with us is that the precious Holy Spirit would dwell in us! Look at First Corinthians: "...*Your body is the temple of the Holy Spirit who is in you...*" (1 Cor. 6:19). So my question is this: Where is the Holy Spirit right now? He is in every believer of Jesus Christ. My point here is that the Holy Spirit is in you right now. If you are born again, or born from above, the giftings of the Holy Spirit are also inside of you. They are gifts of grace; you freely have them. One aspect of our "eternal inheritance" is angels and the ability to co-labor with the Lord's angelic hosts.

That also includes the gift of discerning of spirits. The anointing and ability to see into the realm of angels is already in every believer! The gift just needs to be activated. Bob and Steve's testimonies are great examples of this (see 1 Cor. 12:10; John 14:26). It is possible that Steve's experience under the open heaven at the park near his house played a role in Steve's ability to see angels like the one in the last testimony. These testimonies illustrate how an open heaven can activate a person's innate gift to see into the spiritual realm and the angels therein. So again, I want to encourage you to seek to rend the heavens over your life or to seek out a geographical location where the heavens are already opened and invest in a season of prayer and seeking the face of Christ there.

Kathy had an awesome angelic encounter in Montana that illustrates that open heavens often lead to sightings of angels that are released from the heavens on missions of mercy.

KATHY BASCONI'S ANGELIC ENCOUNTER

In April 2004, Kevin and I were visiting a friend, Dunkin Hill, on his 625-acre ranch in Montana. Our friend was building a log cabin for the Lord on the acreage. We were walking around the house, praying and anointing the log structure with oil. I finished praying, and our friend and I were waiting for Kevin to come around. I looked up and saw a huge angel coming down from an open heaven toward the roof of the cabin. The angel was about 20 feet tall. He had flowing white hair and was clothed in a white robe with a beautiful belt wrapped around his waist. The angel radiated the majesty and beauty of the Lord all around him. His entire body seemed to glisten with the most beautiful, pure, radiant white light. He descended and tucked or folded in his huge wings and went through the roof into the cabin.

Kevin ran around from the back of the cabin and yelled at us, "There's an angel standing in the cabin." We could feel the presence of the angel very strongly, and I praised God that He opened our eyes to see this beautiful angelic being. We believed that the angel was released in answer to our prayers and the request of our friend to anoint the cabin for God's use. We had prayed in that manner and asked that the Lord would release an angel to give strength to the ministers that our friend planned to allow to come and stay there for times of refreshing in the Lord.[4]

I believe that Kathy witnessed the heavens open over Duncan's wilderness cabin in Montana. The apostle Peter also saw the heavens open. Also, in Ezekiel we see a biblical example of a person who experienced "visions of God" and saw the heavens open over a certain geographical region.

Now it came to pass in the thirtieth year, in the fourth month, on the fifth day of the month, as I was among the captives by the River Chebar, that the heavens were opened and I saw visions of God (Ezekiel 1:1).

I do not really claim to have perfect understanding of the things or the dynamic of the open heavens that I experienced at 121 Beech Street or other places. However, I do know that, in those times of waiting upon Jesus, I was given a supernatural knowledge of certain details pertaining to Scripture, and I began to experience the manifest realms of Heaven as it would invade my time and space. I praise the Lord for those times, and I wish to give Him all the glory due to His marvelous name. Once the heavens opened over my life, the effects of the open heaven seemed to manifest in every place I traveled to witness about Christ and His Cross.

TRANSFERRING OPEN HEAVENS

Several biblical accounts of open heavens illustrate that they can be transferred from one individual to another. In some small way, I began to see that once the heavens were "rent" or opened in my life, the effects of that opening seemed to impact several people who came into contact with me. The way that people were affected by the open heavens varied from person to person. Some received healing or miracles. Some received an impartation to see and to hear into the spiritual realm. Some received an increased passion for Christ and began to feel the Lord's presence in a tangible way. This last one also included the manifestation of the fragrance of the Lord or other supernatural signs and wonders. Although these are all wonderful in themselves, the other apparent benefit of living under an open heaven was that the grace and favor of the Lord began to manifest in my life. These same kinds of benefits will begin to occur in your life and sphere of influence when you manage to get the heavens opened up over your life, too.

In Acts 10, we see that the open heaven that was upon Jesus apparently attached itself to the apostle Peter. I believe that the fragrance of heaven can attach to someone who is living under an open heaven in the same way that a strong perfume can be transferred from the person who is wearing it to any person in close proximity to them. In other words, open heavens can be transferable and be given or activated from one person to another person in the same way that a common cold can be caught. When you come into contact with an open heaven, you can catch it!

Look at this verse:

> *The next day, as they went on their journey and drew near the city, Peter went up on the housetop to pray, about the sixth hour. Then he became very hungry and wanted to eat; but while they made ready, he fell into a trance and saw heaven opened and an object like a great sheet bound at the four corners, descending to him and let down to the earth* (Acts 10:9-11).

In this passage, we see Peter practicing one of the most important keys to opening the heavens. He is praying and possibly was fasting as well. In addition to this, the apostle Peter is going with the Gospel to another city. So we see that his sphere of influence is expanding. As a result, he experiences a supernatural encounter with the Spirit of God and enters into a trance. Then, the apostle to the Jews begins to see into the spirit. This is again one of the fruits of an open heaven. Not only that, but Peter sees the heaven open, and he hears the Lord speaking to him, giving him directions to break the Law of Moses! Finally the Holy Spirit gives Peter divine instructions for evangelism and prepares him to preach the Cross to a small group of Gentiles.

You will notice that the dynamics of this open heaven encounter are identical to the time that Peter was with Jesus on the Mount of Transfiguration. He saw the heavens open as a result of prayer. In this instance, it was not Christ's prayer that opened the heavens, but his own. However, the results are the same. Peter sees and hears from the heavenly realm in the open heaven, and he also receives supernatural revelations. So again, we see that Peter caught the authority, ability, or understanding of opening the heavens over his life directly from Christ Jesus, who is also our example. We can also open the heavens over our lives in a similar fashion as we have discussed previously. Of course, the apostle John also benefited from the open heavens that were over the Christ.

HEAVENLY FRUIT

Defining an "open heaven" may be helpful at this point. What is an open heaven, and is the concept of an open heaven biblical? A careful study of the Bible reveals that there are certain geographic regions where the heavens appear to be open, like at the Chebar River or a Mahanaim (see Gen. 32:2). So the concept of an open heaven is quite biblical. Remember that, in the Garden of Eden, the heavens were eternally opened for humankind. That is ultimately the goal of the Lord—to restore eternal open heavens to His creation, humankind. In definition, an open heaven is a place where the veil between the earthly realm (or dimension) and the realm of Heaven (or the spiritual dimension) is thin, porous, unlocked, or allowing free access into the heavens and heavenly places.

The fruit or benefits of an open heaven are that we can see, hear, and understand revelatory knowledge from God in a clear and unpolluted manner. At times, this will result in the ability to see, hear, and receive revelation that will allow ordinary folks to loose angelic ministry to impact their spheres of influence upon the earth. These will all help us to live our lives in triumph and victory. In Deuteronomy, the Lord promises us the benefits of an open heaven in the form of His favor. Look at this verse:

The LORD will open to you His good treasure, the heavens,
to give the rain to your land in its season, and to bless all
the work of your hand. You shall lend to many nations,
but you shall not borrow (Deuteronomy 28:12).

God calls an open heaven, *"His good treasure."* The Lord also promises us in Proverbs 25:2: *"It is the glory of God to conceal a matter, but the glory of kings is to search out a matter."* There are times when we need to search out the Lord's good treasures of open heavens.

Open heavens always result in God's favor being released upon a person and the ability to search out or step into their God-ordained destinies. As we have seen, the Bible clearly illustrates that the heavens were open over Christ at the beginning of His earthly ministry (see Luke 3:21-23). In fact, Jesus ministered under an open heaven right up until the time that He ascended back into the heavens. On occasion, people nearby Jesus were able to see the open heaven that was upon Christ and also hear from the realm of Heaven, as we have seen previously in Luke 3.

Finally, open heavens are available to everyone, and they can be critical to the ability to recognize angelic activity. Open heavens are also invaluable when it comes to understanding how to co-labor with angels. However, it is also possible for the Lord to open the eyes of a person to see angels at any time and at any place. This, of course, is the sovereignty of God!

In the next chapter, I want to share a powerful testimony of open heavens and angelic activity that was used to rend the heavens over a city and region in northwest Tanzania.

ENDNOTES

1. Bob Cegelis and family.

2. Steve Asbury, Bluefield, Virginia.

3. You can find numerous biblical principles that can help unlock the ministry of angels in your life in my previous book.

4. Kathy Basconi.

Chapter 8

OPEN HEAVENS RELEASE A MIRACLE EXPLOSION IN BEUCELECELLI, TANZANIA

This testimony illustrates how the Lord manifested in the most powerful way that I have ever experienced in all of my trips to Africa. In the crusade meeting described in this chapter, I outline how the heavens opened and released the incredible, miracle-working power of God. This was similar to the instance in Luke 5:17 where *"...the power of the Lord was present to heal them."* This testimony also helps to define the way that the Lord will open the heavens over a person's life and allow him or her to have an expanding sphere of influence. I have continued to seek updates from this region concerning the power and demonstration of the Kingdom that was released when the Lord employed angelic ministry to open the heavens there. The events described in this chapter continue to impact that region of Tanzania for God's glory today. It illustrates how God can open the heavens over an individual's life and then use him or her to impact other regions and even nations for Christ's Kingdom.

In February of 2006, I traveled to a small city in the bush of northwest Tanzania, called Beucelecelli. This region has an estimated population of 40,000, with many others living in the surrounding area. Beucelecelli is fairly close to Rwanda. Bishop Zenobius Isaya had arranged this open air soul-winning outreach, and I was not aware of the extent that we would need to travel to reach our destination. The trip to Beucelecelli involved a two-hour boat ride and then a long, bone-jarring, six-hour drive over grueling roads to reach the city. I was exhausted when we did make it to the town and decided to rest and pray.

LET IT RAIN

The heavens were truly brass over my head, and it seemed that I could not get any breakthrough in prayer. In addition to this, I was feeling a considerable amount of opposition in the spirit. I felt the need for some fasting. Isaya came to my room in the evening and told me that the host pastors were requesting to meet with me for dinner. However, I declined their invitation, telling Isaya that I felt the need for fasting and prayer. I prayed nearly all night and did not get any real breakthrough. When the sun came up the next morning, I did not have any clear direction for the ministry for the first night of the meetings, so I continued to fast and pray. About two in the afternoon, I finally heard from the Lord. The Holy Spirit told me, "I want you to stand up on the platform and tell the people that the God you serve, Jesus Christ, is real, He is alive, and Jesus says to tell you that we will see the rain fall on these crusade meetings before we leave your city."

I said, "OK, Lord, but you know that people will not stand in the rain to hear the Gospel." So I was a little concerned with these unexpected directions. When Isaya came to get me to go to the meeting, I was glad to see about 4,000 people waiting on the meeting grounds. They were hungry to hear the Gospel. The first thing that I did was to stand up and declare with as much confidence as I could muster, "The God I serve, Jesus Christ of Nazareth, is real, He is alive, and Jesus says to tell you that we will see the rain fall on these crusade meetings before we leave your city." I was later told that I was the first *wuzungo mhubiri,* or white preacher, to ever preach a healing outreach in the city. The Lord was faithful, and we saw several dozen miracles that night as we declared the Gospel of the Kingdom. There were also several hundred who responded to the altar call to be born again. They prayed to receive Jesus as their Savior and Lord. I had thought it to be a very good night. That is, until I met with the host pastors for dinner after the meeting.

I went to my hostel, took a quick sink bath, and met the pastors. The very first thing that the main pastor said through the interpretation of Isaya was, "You are a very brave and bold man!"

That caught me off guard, and I said, "I am?"

"Yes," he said, "you have stood on the platform in the full view of the whole public and everyone, and you have promised the people that it will rain on my city. It has not rained here for 11 months, and we are in severe famine." When my new friend told me this, I suddenly lost my appetite and quietly decided that I would eat little, and that I would continue to give myself to prayer and fasting. Later, when Isaya and I were alone, the bishop told me that some of the pastors were concerned for my safety. It seemed they felt that some of the Muslims in the city might seek to stone me as a "false prophet" if it did not, in fact, rain within the next two days. This gave me reason to pause and press into the Kingdom of God all the more!

I returned to prayer in my small hostel and again found the heavens "brass" over my head. Sometimes it is just better to worship! I had brought my portable CD player and began to earnestly worship the Lord. I chose the Michael W. Smith song, "Let It Rain." Yes, that was exactly what I needed. I needed the floodgates of Heaven to open up and for God to pour out, not only rain in the natural, but also His presence in the Spirit. I prayed and worshiped all night. When the sun came up, the sky was as clear as a bell, and the bright, hot African sun pierced the flimsy blue curtains of my hostel room. I went to God in prayer again.

"Lord, You told me yesterday to tell these people that it was going to rain on this city. Lord, do You know that it has not rained here for 11 months?" (Of course, He knew.) I struggled in prayer all day. I was concerned and was asking for a miracle in the form of rain. During this time, the Michael W. Smith song "Let It Rain" was repeating on my portable CD player and my mini speakers! About one in the afternoon I began to hear a sound— *thud, thud, thud.* Suddenly, the sound multiplied! Huge rain drops started falling on the metal roof of my hostel—*thud, thud, thud.* Suddenly, there was an earsplitting crack of thunder, and a bolt of lightning lit up the street in front of my room. A lightning bolt had hit a home in the center of Beucelecelli, and the rain was falling in buckets. It was an instant deluge. Torrential rain began to fall from the cloud burst. I have never seen it rain so hard, with the one exception of the time I rode out a hurricane in the Virgin Islands. This downpour was what meteorologists might call a microburst.

I jumped to my feet to dance, but I could not hear the Michael W. Smith song "Let It Rain," because the rain was pounding so heavily upon the tin roof! I turned the volume on my little stereo up as loud as it would go and began to dance and sing before the Lord with all of my heart! Let it rain! Let it rain! Open the floodgates of Heaven! Glory to God in the highest! It was pouring rain; I had never seen anything like this in my life! It rained so hard that water actually began to stream in under the door of my hostel room. To my astonishment, I heard people laughing and dancing in the streets. When I looked out the window of the room, the people of Beucelecelli were dancing in the streets. They had buckets, pails, and any other containers that would collect the water and were celebrating the deluge! I was starting to think that I knew how Noah must have felt. The atmosphere was electric, and you could sense that there had been a dramatic shift in the spiritual climate over the city and region. The heavens had opened over Beucelecelli (see Deut. 28:12). I believe that God had released a "signs and wonders" or "harvester" angel, who had stepped into the village of Beucelecelli at the instant that the lightning bolt struck. The ear-splitting thunder and instantaneous lightning bolt was a sign in the natural of the breaking open of the heavens in the spiritual realm.

Somewhere around 3:00 P.M., I began to realize that if it kept raining like this, the second night of the crusade might well be canceled. Again, I decided that it would be a good time to return to prayer and have some dialogue with my Father. "Lord," I began, "You know if it keeps raining like this the people will not come to hear the Gospel, and if they do not come to hear the Gospel, then not many will be saved today." I continued like this for some time. The heavy rain continued to fall, relentlessly pounding the tin roof. I knew that Isaya was busy keeping our equipment dry and making alternate plans, so I decided not to bother him with a call. The supernatural microburst continued unabated for another hour. By now, the crusade was one hour late getting started.

About 4:30 P.M., the Lord spoke to me and said, "Isaya will call you at 5:14. When he calls, he will tell you that he is on the way to get you. Be ready; I am going to do something special in this city today. I am going to reveal My glory here. You will not have much time to preach, so when you stand on the platform, put on your sunglasses and tell the people this, 'The God I serve, Jesus Christ of Nazareth, is real, He is alive, and Jesus says to tell you that the sun will shine on this crusade meeting today, and we will see mighty miracles of God.'"

In my heart I thought, *Awesome!* In my mind I thought, *Boy, it sure is raining awfully hard!*

At exactly 5:14, my phone rang and it was Isaya telling me that he was on the way to get me. When I arrived at the soccer grounds where the meetings were being held, it was still raining heavily. I was astonished to see an estimated 4,000 people were standing in the downpour waiting to hear the Gospel. I had been in dozens of crusade meetings up to then and had never seen a crowd stand in the rain to hear the Gospel in Africa! When Isaya handed me the microphone, I stepped up to the platform and reaching into my pocket, put on my sunglasses and told the people, "The God I serve, Jesus Christ of Nazareth, is real, He is alive, and Jesus says to tell you people that the sun will shine on this crusade meeting, and we will see mighty miracles of God today!"

I began to preach, and within 15 minutes the dark, overcast sky began to subside a little, although the rain was still falling very hard. There I was with my sunglasses on, peering out through the rain drops. Within my heart, I was praying for God to show up as I preached His Word. The rain slowly let up by degrees. Five minutes later, one single, lone sunbeam instantaneously cracked the sky, and a brilliant stroke of sunshine fell upon the crusade grounds. The lone sunbeam cut through the darkness like a laser and illuminated only the soccer stadium and the crusade grounds.

SIGNS AND WONDERS

I let out a sigh of relief, and to my astonishment, I could see a perfect circle in the clouds above. I could actually see the open heaven over the city. This display of God's glory was almost identical to the way that I had seen the heavens open over the Sara Creasy Metcalf Amphitheater in Bluefield, Virginia, in 2003 with Steve Asbury. The supernatural sunbeam fell at about an 80-degree angle, hitting the grounds. All around the rest of the area it was still dark and raining heavily. To my amazement, when the brilliantly bright sunbeam fractured the dark sky, people began to pour into the crusade grounds. Within five minutes, several thousand more people appeared out of nowhere and doubled the number of people who were on hand. A few minutes later, I was just about to give an altar call to receive Jesus Christ as Savior when Wade Holland broke my train of thought. Wade was tugging frantically, pulling on my wet white suit jacket sleeve. I turned to see what in the world it was about, only to find him pointing excitedly at the sky directly above the platform and the altar.

What a glorious sign and wonder the Lord had given the wonderful, precious people of Beucelecelli. I turned to see the most magnificent double rainbow that I have ever witnessed. It was so close that I felt that I could reach out and break off a piece and taste it! Immediately, the Holy Spirit took over the meeting. I told the people of Beucelecelli that God had given them a sign in the heavens. I said that no white preacher can make it rain or make the sun shine; only God in Heaven could do those things. I told the people about Noah, and how God gave Noah a covenant but that we had a better covenant in Christ Jesus! The atmosphere had broken open, and the power of God was now present to heal (see Luke 5:17). I could feel the healing anointing in the air. The hair on my left arm stood on end, and I knew that the healing angel was nearby. In fact, I was certain that an army of God's angelic hosts had invaded the city! I never saw the healing angel or any other angels in Beucelecelli. However, I could sense their presence extremely strongly. The effects of the angel's presence and the accompanying power of God to heal were released as the heavens opened, and those effects were soon to be witnessed by all those who were present on the grounds.

I told the people if they wanted to be born again and to have a covenant relationship with Jesus Christ the Son of the Living God to respond by coming to the altar. An estimated 4,000 quickly came forward to pray to receive Jesus. After I led them in the prayer of salvation, I found these words coming out of my mouth: "The message and preaching of the Cross is foolishness to those who are perishing and going to burn for eternity in hell, but to those who are being saved, to those who are going to inherit eternal life in Heaven and paradise, it is the power of God! The power of God is here to heal! We are going to see God do mighty miracles now!"

At that instant, there was a crack of loud thunder, and then I heard a scream. Suddenly, many people began to scream! The glory of God multiplied, and immediately hundreds of people began to violently manifest demons. The pastors and ushers worked as best they could to drag the demonized to the rear of the platform, but there were just too many possessed by devils. I knew that the power of God was present to heal and to deliver, just like in Luke 5:17. I began to call out healing after healing. The new converts began to literally throw the demonized people onto the platform! I commanded this to stop, but they continued to throw people onto the platform anyway. The meeting seemed to be spiraling out of control!

For a few moments, things got a bit out of hand. I like to keep order on the platform, and I was trying to get some of the people whom I knew had been healed to come to the platform and give their testimonies. However, they just kept throwing people on the platform. Suddenly, I realized they were throwing the ones who had been healed onto the platform. Blind eyes had opened, deaf ears had been opened, and tumors had dissolved. There were people all over the place. "Isaya," I bellowed, "what are these three men doing on the platform? I only want those who are healed up here!"

"They can hear!" he replied.

"What do you mean?" I asked.

"These three men could not hear. They were, for sure, totally deaf, but now, sir, praise God, they do hear well!" We started to get the testimonies from the three deaf men who Jesus had sovereignly healed, when out of the corner of my eye something caught my attention. By now, the people were screaming and miracles were happening all over the crusade grounds. Thousands had just been saved, and the power of God was now present to heal anyone willing to reach out and touch the hem of Jesus' garment. Jesus was sovereignly releasing mighty miracles and healings to the people of Beucelecelli under the open heaven The Holy Spirit was present in power and God's angelic host seemed to be working in symphony and harmony with the Holy Ghost to release Christ's Kingdom in power!

Now I saw a man walking in my direction with both of his arms stretched out in front of him as if he were seeking to reach out and touch me. His appearance and the way in which he was walking made me feel quite uncomfortable. He was walking like the monster from one of those old Frankenstein movies. I saw him come from all the way across the stage, and I could see that he was having some trouble keeping his balance as he stepped over and between the writhing bodies that were littering the platform. Streams of tears were flowing from his eyes. "Isaya," I shrieked, "what is this guy doing up here?" pointing at the "Frankenstein" man. As Isaya spoke to him, I took a second to grab a drink of water and peek behind the platform, where there were hundreds of people violently manifesting demons. Most of the pastors and ushers were busy with deliverance, yelling and commanding the devils to come out in Swahili.

This was the Kingdom of God manifest upon the earth! *Awesome,* I thought, *the Lord has manifested His glory and the kingdom of darkness is coming out of people! God's Kingdom has come!* I saw my friend, Wade Holland, sitting behind me, and yelled at him over the din of noise, "Wade, get back there and cast out all those demons!"

Wade looked at me a little dumbfounded, as if to say, "Me, cast out demons?"

"Get back there," I ordered, and he jumped up and waded into the fray of writhing, demonized people behind the platform. Wade did succeed in casting out a lot of devils that evening in the name of Jesus. However, later he told me that there was one woman whom he could not get delivered. She was levitating or actually floating about eighteen inches off of the ground and writhing like a snake. The whites of her eyes were red, and the pupils of her eyes were white. This poor woman's tongue appeared to be split as it poked in and out of her mouth. I saw Wade later as the meeting was winding up. He sort of "walked" the levitating, demonized woman around behind the platform with his hand on her throat commanding the devils within her to come out in Jesus' name.

Miracles were happening left and right. Now the man who had been walking like Frankenstein was ready to give his testimony. I just handed the microphone to him, and he began to speak in Swahili and Isaya interpreted for me in English. The man said, "I was brought to the meeting today on my mat. As you know, I have been paralyzed from my birth. But when the white preacher said the words, 'The power of God is here to heal,' I felt something like lightning go into my head. Power went into my body, my legs became strong, and I said to myself, 'For sure, Jesus has healed me.' You all know me, but as you can plainly see now, it is true. God has healed me and I can walk, praise God, I can walk. Jesus is alive, for He has healed me!"

It turned out that the man was well known in the city. Many people did, indeed, know who he was. As he shared his testimony, the miracles began to multiply, and it seemed the faith of the people had exploded. Along with their faith came an explosion of miracles! Healing after healing and miracle after miracle manifested. I did not touch anyone. The power of Jesus was, indeed, present to heal. There were hundreds who were healed and hundreds who received miracles. This was the most powerful single healing meeting I have ever personally witnessed. What Jesus did that day in Beucelecelli was truly amazing. God is worthy of all the glory! I touched no one; Jesus Christ healed them all by His finished work of Calvary and through His shed blood!

We had taken the Philadelphia Gospel Assembly Living Waters Choir, from Mwazna, Tanzania, with us to minister in praise and worship. However, the members of choir ended up ministering to those who needed deliverance and casting out many devils. If my memory is correct, the choir saw three deaf-mutes healed through their prayers. We also saw God heal a number of blind people, many deaf people, a few who were paralyzed, numerous tumors, and a multitude of other miracles. We continued to get testimonies of the healings and miracles for nearly two more hours, well into the evening.

At one point, my good friend, Bishop Isaya, was bringing a young woman to me to give her testimony, and he was saying, "Wow, wow, wow, wow, wow!" When I asked him what had happened, he told us that the woman, who appeared to be about 25, had been totally deaf and dumb from birth, but now she could hear and speak. When I asked her to talk and placed the microphone to her lips she shouted, "Wow, wow, wow, wow, wow!" It seemed that "wow" was the first word she had heard Isaya say, and since she had never heard or spoken before, that was the only word that she knew how to speak. We encouraged the mother of the young woman to help teach her how to speak! "Wow, wow, wow, wow, wow!" Now, when we have a great miracle in the open air meetings that we conduct in Africa, we sometimes let one another know that God has worked a great miracle by saying, "Wow, wow, wow, wow, wow!"

The next night the meeting grew, and there were over 10,000 on the grounds because the testimonies of the power of God and the miracles and healings traveled by word of mouth throughout the bush, and many people came to Beucelecelli from the outlying villages. The Lord moved in power the third and final night of the crusade meetings. Although the level of the miracles and healings was very high, there was no comparison to the miracles, deliverances, and healings from the second night when the Lord had so dramatically opened the heavens over the region. On the other hand, we did see several thousand receive Jesus Christ as Savior the last night. The biggest complaint I remember about the ministry in the city was from one pastor whose church went from 40 to 700 members overnight. He was upset because he did not have enough room for them all! Here is Isaya's testimony of the meetings in Beucelecelli.

ISAYA'S TESTIMONY

Wow, wow, wow, wow, wow! A big smile does, indeed, come to my face when I do fondly remember our powerful time of preaching in Beucelecelli. They do, in fact, wish for King of Glory to be returning for a new crusade in the city. The pastors did also, at first, think that maybe evangelist Kevin may not been in right mind after first night. This is because he was bold in Jesus to tell the people that it would, in fact, rain on the city of Beucelecelli. For sure, at that time it had been some long time until it had rained in the city, and there was actual big problem with no water for drinking, animals, and also the people suffer much with crops. But our God is faithful. It did, for sure, rain very much.

We did, in fact, see a great sign in the heaven. A big rainbow did come to stand behind the platform as we did preach about Jesus and His salvation. In fact, there were two rainbows beside one another. Then God did, in fact, come and prove that He is, in fact, real and there many,

many who were healed from their sickness and demons that night. This was just like it may have been in old Bible times. One man, who was a paralytic from his birth, was also healed, and did, in fact, walk across platform to give a great testimony of Jesus. This one had not been able to walk before, some 38 years from the time that he was born, and was, in fact, known in the city. When he did share his testimony there were many who also had their faith built up to receive from God also.

I shall always fondly remember the deaf mute woman who was totally healed at the altar of salvation. She never, in fact, had the ability to hear or to speak at all before this day. So she did not know any words. She did not know Swahili and English—it also escapes her. So when we did ask for the testimony, she could only shout out, "Wow, wow, wow, wow, wow!" I am, indeed, smiling even as I do write to you now. What a great miracle that we did see with this woman. We were much blessed, and also the pastors of Beucelecelli, as many had their churches grow while we visited the city. Many, many people made the decision to live for Jesus, and the church did get a great victory. Now, no one in Beucelecelli can say our God is not alive, for He did, in fact, reveal Himself to the whole city! Many, many deaf were, in fact, healed by the power of God. Many blind were also healed, and many, many that suffer with tumors were also delivered and made whole by God Himself. There were, in fact, very many other miracles and healings also happened in the meetings, and it is too much to remember them all! But

I shall always remember the deaf mute woman who told us, "Wow, wow, wow, wow, wow!" What a great miracle she did receive from Jesus. Praise our God for He is good![1]

WADE HOLLAND'S TESTIMONY

In February 2006, I traveled to Mwanza, Tanzania, to help Kevin Basconi work on an orphanage. I arrived in Mwanza about a week after Kevin, and I caught a bus to Beucelecelli to join him in a healing crusade there. But nothing could ever prepare me for what I was about to experience in those meetings when I arrived in Beucelecelli. The first night went well, with many healings, signs, and wonders. It had been very dry, and there had been no rain for months, but Kevin said God the Father promised rain before the crusade was done. Wow, you could have cut the heavens with a knife as we went up on the rooftop lounge to have supper. It was no wonder Kevin did not eat that first night when he finished meeting with the pastors, and they told him that they feared for his safety. I know that Kevin indeed hears from the Father, but to promise rain was a big leap of faith. We finished supper and went to our rooms. Kevin said, "Pray that I heard the Lord correctly!"

Thanks a lot, Kevin! I did not get very much sleep that night thinking about what might happen if it did not rain. The next morning, Bishop Isaya came and got me for breakfast and then dropped me back at my room. I decided to worship the Lord, and I turned on my mp3 player. I lay down on my bed to pray and fell fast asleep. I awoke some time later to the sound of water, and I thought that I had left the shower turned on. When I tried to take a shower earlier, I found out the water was shut off for the day due to the drought. I jumped to my feet, thinking, *Great! I will have a shower to cool off.* However, it was not the shower. I realized it was indeed raining, and quite hard at that. I went out to the front of the building to watch the rain, and as fast as it started, it quit. I turned to go back into my room, and all of a sudden there was a crack of thunder like I had never heard before and it started to pour. It was raining so hard that it was running in under the doors of the rooms we were staying in.

The people of the city were screaming and shouting and dancing in the streets. What a time they were having! I returned to my room and once again started to pray and praise the Lord. I kept singing, "Let it rain; let it rain." Kevin had said we were going to the crusade grounds early, but at 4:00, I still had not heard from him and the rain was still coming. Another half hour passed, and there was still no word and it was still raining hard. I wondered, *Are we going to have the meeting in the rain?* I met Bishop Isaya in the hallway around 5:00. He was on his way to pick up Kevin. He was all excited; there were people waiting at the grounds for the meeting. I thought that it was funny when Kevin opened the door, all dressed in his white African suit, because he had sunglasses on, but there was no sun shining outside and it was dark and overcast. Kevin asked me where my sunglasses were. I said in my room. He said, "Get them, because you will need them."

He told me that God said there would be sunshine on the platform. I was not going to argue; after all, he had said God said it was going to rain, and it was indeed raining. We arrived at the grounds, and there were thousands of people standing in the rain waiting to hear the Gospel.

The choir stopped singing, and Bishop Isaya spoke for a minute and then handed Kevin the microphone. You have to picture Kevin wearing a white suit that's soaking wet from the pouring rain and wearing dark sunglasses as he steps up to the front of the platform to start speaking. Just before he started, he turned around and looked at us sitting at the back of the platform and smiled. I will never forget that smile. Then he turned to the crowd and screamed, "Praise the Lord" in Swahili and thanked the Lord for the rain and thanked the thousands for coming and waiting in the rain to hear the Gospel. Kevin went on and told everybody on the grounds that God was going to do even more miracles tonight than the night before and that God said that He was going to make the sun shine on the meetings that evening.

Kevin also told the people that he was instructed not to pray for anyone—that God Himself was going to do the healings and miracles. Kevin then asked if there were any out in crowd of people who were not saved and who wanted to receive Jesus Christ as Lord and Savior. Many stepped forward, and Kevin led them in the prayer of salvation. It was at this time when all of a sudden a bright flash of light struck the platform, so bright even our sunglasses were not enough to stop us from being momentarily blinded by it. As Kevin prayed with the people I had to look away, and when I did I saw this beautiful double rainbow. It was magnificent, and I had never seen anything like it before in my life. I can only imagine what it was like for Noah back in the Old Testament when God sent the rainbow as a covenant that He would never flood the earth with water again.

I had to show this to Kevin, so I rushed across the platform and started tugging on Kevin's sleeve. I was pointing to the sky. I have heard the saying "every color of the rainbow," but I have never seen the colors repeat one on top of the other before. I kept pointing toward the sky, saying, "You need to see this." Kevin looked up and quickly called the people's attention to this supernatural marvel. As he did, he described it to the thousands of people crowded into the meeting grounds. The rain had stopped, so many people were coming out, and he told the people that the double rainbow was indeed a sign from the Father God, just like the days of Noah, and it was a sign that God was sending His healing angels to walk among them.

I am not sure how many stepped forward, because as soon as Kevin started to lead the people in prayer, everything went crazy. That is the only way to describe it. It was chaos. People were screaming and falling down everywhere. The pastors were throwing people on the platform and carrying people away. To say things got out of hand for a few minutes is an understatement. It took Kevin some time to get things back to some sort of almost-control. Kevin kept saying over and over, "I do not want anyone on the platform. I am not laying hands on anyone or praying for anyone. This is God's hour; we only want testimonies from those whom God has healed." Kevin said, "Bishop Isaya, what is that woman doing up here? Get her off the platform."

Bishop Isaya told him, "But Kevin, God has healed her. She was blind, but now she can see."

Later, I remember Kevin telling me to go behind the platform and help the pastors cast out demons. So I went off the platform and began to pray for the demonized. There were dozens of people violently manifesting demons. What a time I had! We cast out many, many demons from a whole lot of people. I remember one incident that still gives me the chills. There was one demon-possessed woman who the pastors had bound by her hands and feet. This was because she was so supernaturally strong as the demons that were possessing her manifested. She had overpowered five full-grown men.

I could not believe my eyes. On my television at home, several times I had seen illusionists do a levitation trick where they would have a woman lay on a table and then remove the table and the woman would not fall. They would pass hoops around her. However, I never expected to see someone levitate in real life. This woman was hovering completely off the ground, and the only things holding her there were the restraints the pastors had put on her. As we cast out demon after demon and bound the spirit of witchcraft, she slowly lowered till she was lying on the ground. I spent a long time praying for her deliverance. Later, when Kevin called me to come to the car as we were done for the night, I was still praying for her, and she was still growling like a wild animal.

The local pastors continued to minister to this woman after the crusade. As it turned out she was a practicing witch doctor who had come to the meetings with the intention of disrupting them. We were told later that she received a great deal of freedom and was born again. She is now a member of a local church and is learning to walk with Jesus.

What an unbelievable time I had there in Beucelecelli! Nothing could have prepared me for that event in my life. I am still waiting for the time when Father God will allow me to experience His angelic presence in that magnitude again. When the glory of God fell, God's angels showed up and the demons had to flee! The third night of the meeting went very well with many saved and healed, but it did not compare to the second night when God's power and glory fell after the rain. As we left the city the morning after the third meeting, the sky was gray and threatening to rain. As we left in the morning for the six-hour drive back to the ferry on Lake Victoria, the rain started to fall gently again. I thought to myself, "This city will never be the same."[2]

The testimonies in these last two chapters will help to broaden your horizon and mindset concerning the appearance of angels. I have included them to help you understand that angels come in an incredible variety of shapes and sizes. The Lord's angels also have a multitude of duties and affect the realms of earth in a much more complicated and sophisticated ways than many of us first conceive or understand, especially as we first begin to learn about the angelic realm from our Bible studies. Certainly, the testimonies of angelic ministry in the canon of Scripture are much more complex than first meets the eye. Often as we read the Bible, we miss the enormity and extravagance of angelic visitations and their impact upon the stories that we take for granted in the Word of God.

A good example of this is found in Exodus 13. It is possible that the Lord's angels played a role in the pillar of cloud by day or the pillar of fire by night. Certainly the angel that rolled away the stone from Christ's tomb was truly powerful and majestic. We see this briefly described in Matthew:

> *There was a great earthquake; for an angel of the Lord descended from heaven, and came and rolled back the stone from the door, and sat on it. His countenance was like lightning, and his clothing as white as snow* (Matthew 28:2-3).

Remember that the earthquake was so intense that the temple was shaken and swayed with the intensity of the quake. As we near the triumphant return of the Lord, the world will begin to witness an accelerated manifestation of Christ's Kingdom. Many of these extraordinary angelic visitations will be especially remarkable because of their demonstrations of the supernatural aspects of the Lord's Kingdom. This last testimony illustrates how some angelic visitations will be overpowering and extravagant in their demonstration of Christ's Kingdom. In subsequent testimonies,

I share an incredible set of individuals' testimonies of one such manifestation of the mystical aspects of the Kingdom of God and His angelic hosts! Next, we will look at simple ways to maintain open heavens over your life.

ENDNOTES

1. Bishop Zenobius Isaya, Philadelphia Gospel Assembly, Mwanza, Tanzania.

2. Wade Holland, Hannah, Alberta, Canada.

Chapter 9

MAINTAINING OPEN HEAVENS OVER YOUR LIFE

The prophet Isaiah made a remarkable and prophetic request of God Almighty in Isaiah 64:

> *Oh, that You would rend the heavens! That You would come down! That the mountains might shake at Your presence—as fire burns brushwood, as fire causes water to boil—to make Your name known to Your adversaries, that the nations may tremble at Your presence!* (Isaiah 64:1-2)

This is a bold decree. Actually, it is a prayer that asks for God to open the heavens and manifest Himself. It is a cry for the very presence of God to visit us. It is a desperate statement that is full of truth and pregnant with prophetic promises. Isaiah is weeping and asking the Lord to open the heavens. The result is that the very earth might be shaken by the presence of Almighty God.

Abraham was a friend of God who had this experience in Genesis 17:

> *When Abram was ninety-nine years old, the LORD appeared to Abram and said to him, "I am Almighty God; walk before Me and be blameless"* (Genesis 17:1).

What we are really talking about is becoming a friend of God. We are actually asking for the presence of God to refine us and burn away everything that is within us that is not of Him. Some call this the Refiner's Fire (see Mal. 3:2-3; 1 Peter 4:12). As a result of submitting to the Refiner's Fire, the friends of God walk under an open heaven much like Adam and Eve in the Garden.

So from my personal experience, I can say that getting the heavens opened over my life was the first step in becoming a friend of God. This was a process and took a season of time. The progression of opening the heavens was accelerated by radical obedience to the Holy Spirit. This is not always easy and requires that you walk blamelessly before God. During this process, the Holy Spirit will frequently ask you to do things that seem impossible. These prophetic acts often do not make a lot of sense to our carnal minds. However, it is critical that we are obedient to the slightest leadings of the Lord. We must purpose in our hearts and minds to seek God no matter what the cost. Usually the Lord will require us to give Him something that will cost us dearly in one way or another. But it is absolutely necessary to be obedient in these areas. Once the heavens are open over your life, there is no guarantee that they will remain open. You will need to be diligent to maintain your open heaven. You will need to water your open heaven with a lifestyle of prayer, repentance, and obedience.

MAINTAINING THE OPEN HEAVEN

I have called these requests from the Lord prophetic acts of obedience. These things are nothing new in the Kingdom of God. I am sure that you are well aware of the substantial track record that is contained in the canon of Scripture concerning unusual acts of obedience by friends of God. Ezekiel is a good biblical example of a person who was required to perform some unusual prophetic acts. However, the canon of Scripture is littered with folks the God of the universe asked to do some weird things. He may require you to do a few odd things in your quest for an open heaven, too (see Ezek. 4:1-12).

Let me just sum this up by saying that God may ask you to march around the walls of Jericho seven times before they come tumbling down. Incidentally, the story of Jericho is a great parabolic picture of how God may choose to open the heavens over your life (see Josh. 6:4-15)! The impenetrable walls of the fortified city of Jericho can be a perfect representation of the heavens over a person's life. The heavens over your head may seem impenetrable in your current circumstances and geographic location, but once again, remember that with God nothing is impossible. That is why it is absolutely imperative that we are obedient to the Spirit of God. Even if He tells us to march around in a circle seven times and shout or be immersed seven times while being baptized or to give away all of your earthly possessions, we need to be obedient to the Lord in things like these if we truly desire to live under an open heaven. Incidentally, the Lord has asked me to do all of the above!

I am outlining several keys that can help you to rend the heavens over your life. It is important to be obedient to the Lord in these things, as it is only God who has the ability and authority to open the heavens over your life. So the first and most important step is to be obedient to the Lord in *all* aspects of your life. Let me say this another way. Repent! You must cease from sin and turn away from it. Sin in your life will clog up the heavens over your life once you get them open. Again, one key to rend or open the heavens over your life is to walk blamelessly with God. This is called friendship or communion.

Briefly, this can also be a process. Allow me to open up for a moment. Thankfully, the Lord is merciful and kind. He is patient with us and will often give us years to cease from sinful behavior. During this refining process, the Holy Spirit will be wooing you and convicting you of any behavior that is unpleasant in the Lord's sight. Most people, myself included, are not able to stop sinning immediately upon receiving Christ as Savior. Some folks call this cleansing work of the Holy Spirit sanctification. In all honesty, I still have areas the Holy Spirit is refining in my life. I am a work in progress. I was willing to stop the sinful behavior in my life. The Lord was gracious and delivered me from my sinful lifestyle in a gradual way. Profanity, deceit or lying, coveting, jealousy, envy, murdering others with my words, hypocrisy, lust, and sexual immorality were all things that the Lord has helped me to overcome since I have been walking with Him. (This is actually a very short list of my shortcomings, as there were a bunch). The point I want to make is that God is very patient with us, and the Holy Spirit will help us and patiently cleanse us from all unrighteousness in the refining fire or forge of God.

Romans illustrates the sinful human or unrighteous nature that we need to overcome:

> *Being filled with all unrighteousness, sexual immoral-*
> *ity, wickedness, covetousness, maliciousness; full of envy,*

murder, strife, deceit, evil-mindedness; they are whisper-
ers, backbiters, haters of God, violent, proud, boasters,
inventors of evil things, disobedient to parents, undiscern-
ing, untrustworthy, unloving, unforgiving, unmerciful;
who, knowing the righteous judgment of God, that those
who practice such things are deserving of death, not only
do the same but also approve of those who practice them
(Romans 1:29-32).

Thank God that we have an Advocate, and the Lord is patient and willing to forgive us of any of the sins and unrighteous behaviors that are listed above.

The key is to confess our sins and ask for His help. We must desire to change. When we make that heart decision to change, He promised to not only forgive us of our sin but to cleanse us from all unrighteousness! God has also promised to forget our sins (see Ps. 103:12). So, according to the principle of First John, we can be restored to a right relationship or friendship with the Lord, *"If we confess our sins, He is faithful and just to forgive us our sins and to cleanse us from all unrighteousness"* (1 John 1:9). God will cleanse us, and this is a very important step to rending the heavens over your life and also to maintaining your open heaven. As humans, we can sin unwittingly on a daily basis. That is why a lifestyle of repentance is very important when seeking to open your heavens. Repentance is a very important key to maintaining the open heavens over your life.

Remember that Jesus was in the process of being baptized when the heavens opened over His life at the age of 30. Christ's submission to John the Baptist's ministry of baptism was an act of obedience. When Jesus practiced this principle, the heavens opened over

His life. We know that the Christ was blameless and without sin (see Heb. 4:15). Jesus modeled the process of opening the heavens with an act of repentance by obediently submitting to John the Baptist's ministry, and we need to emulate His example.

So, rending the heavens over your life is the first step to walking under an open heaven. We see from the life of Christ that both obedience and repentance are crucial to this process. However, the heavens over you can open in several ways. You can find a geographical place where the heavens are truly open and invest time seeking the Lord there and practice the tools or keys to opening the heavens over your life. When the Lord spoke to me to travel to Newfoundland, Canada, in the middle of the winter, He was positioning me in a place where He knew the heavens would be open. The Lord also knew that I would have the opportunity to experience the effects of the open heaven there. So the Lord had me travel to a specific geographic region where He had preordained that the heavens would be open. I experienced an open heaven for the first time by proximity, just like many folks in the Bible.

AN OPEN HEAVEN LIFE

As I have stated, this series of events transformed my life. I was given a divine understanding of my need to repent and draw closer to God. However, when I returned to my hometown in America, the heavens were brass overhead (see Deut. 28:23). The heavens were impenetrable over the little house at 121 Beech Street compared to the wonderful experiences I had walked through in Canada under the open heavens there. So I began to bombard the heavens there with prayer, repentance, fasting, and a gritty determination to rend the heavens over my head. It took about three months of continually pressing into the Kingdom of God before I began to get a breakthrough. After I obtained a victory and got a little crack in the spiritual realm over my little house on Beech Street, I began to discern a little angelic activity there. From that point, I redoubled my efforts to break through. Soon I began the process of entertaining heaven and God's angels until the Holy Spirit fell in power. When that happened the heavens were blasted open by the Holy Ghost. Remember, it is God alone who is responsible for opening the heavens over a person's life and sphere of influence. So we must be diligent and determined.

This pursuit of God's Kingdom, the Holy Spirit, and open heavens became a ceaseless lifestyle for me. Therefore, I purposed in my heart to rend the gates of Heaven over my life and seek Christ's face until the glory fell. I purposed within my heart to take the Kingdom of Heaven by violence. I did this by a combination of devotions, prayer, fasting, and repentance. You will find a short list of keys at the end of this chapter, which you can easily practice and which will help you rend the heavens over your life and keep them open.

Through the unction or leading of the Holy Spirit, I entertained Heaven. I sought Heaven in my every waking moment. I determined to focus my mind upon Christ and to seek those things that are above (see Isa. 26:3). I had experienced the reality of Heaven and the heavenly places or open heavens. I simply decided that I did not want to live in the delusion, duplicity, and hypocrisy that most people call a normal Christian life. I wanted God. I wanted all of God and everything that was available in His Kingdom now, in this life. In hindsight, I believe that it was, indeed, the Lord Himself who stirred me up to press into His Kingdom with extreme determination, prayer, and fasting. Perhaps the Holy Spirit will use this book to stir up your spirit in a similar manner.

Colossians 3:1-3 became my lifestyle. I purposed in my heart to break into the realms of Heaven. I actually declared to God in prayer on many occasions, "Lord, if You are not going to come down here, then I am going to come up there. I am going to press in. You promised me that if I sought You with all of my heart, that I would find You. So I am seeking you with every fiber of my spirit, soul, and body." I became desperate for more of Him. I unwittingly practiced the prophet Isaiah's prayer found in Isaiah 64. I petitioned God repeatedly to rend the heavens and to come down, just like the persistent widow! I implored the God of Heaven to reveal Himself to me and to open the very heavens over my head and life. This is another tool or Kingdom key that you can also employ according to the principle of Matthew 7:7: *"Ask."*

Asking God for the impossible, my friends, is another important way that can help you open the heavens over your life. God in Heaven rewards desperation, perseverance, and obedience (see James 4:8). Look at Colossians:

> *If then you were raised with Christ, seek those things which are above, where Christ is, sitting at the right hand of God. Set your mind on things above, not on things on the earth. For you died, and your life is hidden with Christ in God* (Colossians 3:1-3).

You may wish to consider making this passage your heart's cry as well. Even as I write this paragraph this evening, the Holy Spirit is whispering to me, "For some of you reading this book, you can accept this promise from the Scripture. You can seek those things which are above. You will find them. Among those heavenly things are the open heavens. You can have them, too." God is ready, willing, and able to open the heavens over your life.

In my first book, I also shared how Christ spoke the words of Jeremiah 29 over my life as He called me into my destiny. That promise is also open to you. Please take this passage from Jeremiah as a prophetic promise for you as you read this book and prepare your heart to rend the heavens over your life. (This is very special; I am writing in a prophetic manner. That is a bit new to me.)

> *For thus says the LORD...I will visit you and perform My good word toward you, and cause you to return to this place* [His presence]. *For I know the thoughts that I think toward you, says the LORD, thoughts of peace and not of evil, to give you a future and a hope. Then you will call upon Me and go and pray to Me, and I will listen to you. And you will seek Me and find Me, when you search for Me with all your heart* (Jeremiah 29:10-13).

The Christ will surely be found by you when you search for Him with all of your heart, all of your soul, and all of your mind. You can bank on it. This is really a promise of the heavens opening over your life. But you need to get real. You need to develop a passion, desperation, and hunger for the heavenly realm. Heaven must become more real to you than the book that you are holding in your hands at this moment. In fact, it is.

We also have the pledge found in John. I find these words of Jesus to be an amazing promise:

> *He who has My commandments and keeps them, it is he who loves Me. And he who loves Me will be loved by My*

Father, and I will love him and manifest Myself to him (John 14:21).

What the Lord is actually saying here is that He will appear to those who love Him and are obedient. Just like the resurrected Christ appeared to the disciples, He has promised to appear to you and me in a similar way. Remember that when Jesus Christ comes, He manifests with an open heaven over Him, and when you see Him you will also be in a position to enter into Christ's open heaven, just like the disciples. The Greek word used here for manifest is *emphanizo*. The literal translation of *emphanizo* can mean to *exhibit* (in person) or *disclose* by appearance, declare plainly, inform, manifest, show, signify, or display.[1] The connotation is the same as to display a fine masterpiece or work of art in a gallery setting.

What a wonderful promise from the Lord. He has promised to visit us and come to tea. That is also another aspect of an open heaven—visitations of the Lord. Once you experience the fruit that comes from living under an open heaven, you will want to camp there. Once you begin to have an intimate friendship with the Lord and the precious Holy Spirit, you will never want to leave that place. Once you rend the heavens over your life, the Lord will open up your spiritual senses. Then you will begin to see, hear, and receive revelations from the heavenly realm on a regular basis. These gifts of the Spirit and supernatural experiences will certainly transform your life, just like they did mine. They will empower and enable you to manifest Christ's Kingdom and His Kingship upon the earth and in your sphere of influence.

Once you get the heavens open in your life, you will need to learn how to maintain them. This requires some discipline.

However, the most important aspect of maintaining open heavens over your head is a love and desire to be with the Lord above all else. There are no shortcuts here. Again, it is important that we follow Jesus' model. Jesus was always obedient to the Father 100 percent of the time. We also need to develop a lifestyle in which we seek to live in obedience to the Holy Spirit and the Father. Remember what Jesus said:

> *Most assuredly, I say to you, the Son can do nothing of Himself, but what He sees the Father do; for whatever He does, the Son also does in like manner* (John 5:19).

We need to emulate the Lord in this passionate desire for obedience. Our goal should be 100 percent obedience 100 percent of the time.

DISCIPLINE AND OBEDIENCE

The Messiah also modeled a lifestyle of fasting and separation unto the Lord. Jesus practiced a lifestyle of prayer and meditation of God's Word. That is why He often withdrew from the press to invest solitary time alone with the Father and the Holy Spirit. Likewise, we also need to discipline ourselves to seek to find time to wait upon God in the secret place. Even after great moves of God and healing revivals, Christ sought times of separation and communion with the Father and the Holy Spirit. We see this aspect of Christ's devotional life illustrated in Mark 6:46: *"And when He had sent them away, He departed to the mountain to pray."* It is important for us to also practice a lifestyle in intimacy and communion with God in our prayer lives, too. Christ retreated from a massive revival that was full of miracles, signs, and wonders to be alone with His Father.

This discipline will play a key role in your ability to maintain an open heaven over your life (see Matt. 14:15,23; Luke 9:10; John 6:15). Investing alone time with the Holy Spirit is absolutely necessary to maintain an open heaven. Jesus separated Himself and made place in the business of His ministry for communion with the Holy Spirit. We must also separate ourselves and follow Christ's example in this. There is no substitute for investing time in waiting or meditative prayer, as in this place we draw close to God. In return He opens the heavens over our lives (see Ps. 4:4; 27:14; 37:7; Isa. 40:31).

At times the Lord may lead you into a wilderness experience. We have seen how this dynamic was used in the life of Jesus, Elijah, Moses, Paul, and to a very small degree, myself, although I do not intend to place myself in the previous category. Far from it; I am but an ordinary person, but my experiences can be a prophetic promise to you, too (see Rev. 19:10). At times, the Lord will actually lead you to separate yourself with Him in a wilderness experience. These times should not be dreaded or avoided. In fact, they should be embraced and enjoyed. Often, when you are called into the wilderness, you will come out in the power of the Spirit with the heavens open over your life. You can rend the heavens open over your own life. At times, you can get your own breakthrough. Or at other times, you can seek a Mahanaim. Find a geographic location where the heavens are already open and invest time seeking the Lord there. This can help you to break through and establish an open heaven over your life (see Gen. 32:2).

If you have the opportunity, you can at times "piggy back" on other folks' breakthroughs and enter into the open heaven by their "up draught." We have seen this kind of breakthrough in the Scriptures in the lives of the disciples who entered into the open heavens that were over Christ. Elisha was able to tap into the supernatural power of God by giving close attention to his teacher, Elijah. Joshua broke through because he served and honored Moses. In modern times, others have entered into the open heavens, or Kingdom of God, through the ministries of folks like Katherine Kuhlman, John Wimber, Maria Woodworth-Etter, William Brannon, and Smith Wigglesworth. The Argentine Revival was sparked when one woman tapped upon a small wooden table and opened the heavens over an entire nation with one simple act of obedience. Today, we also have folks like Bill Johnson, Randy Clark, Roland and Heidi Baker, John and Carol Arnott, and Patricia King who willingly train and teach people how to step into the miraculous and open heavens. It is also true that there are thousands more of the Lord's people with hearts to train you but who are hidden or obscure. So seek out individuals who can help you in one way or another. My prayer is that some of you reading this will break through by these writings and that you will be encouraged to dig your own well.

In conclusion, I would like to encourage you to seek the Lord for yourself. Perhaps, if God in His mercy can transform the life of an ordinary man from the Appalachian Mountains—what many would consider an unqualified hillbilly—then the Lord can also transform your life too. Here is a short list of keys that you can use to open the heavens over your life. As a result, you may begin to receive revelation and authority to co-labor with God's angels as you seek to establish the Kingdom of God in your sphere of influence.

KEYS TO OPENING THE HEAVENS

1. *Prayer.* Ask God. We need to live a lifestyle of ceaseless prayer (see Matt. 21:22; Mark 11:24; John 14:13; 16:23).

2. *Repentance.* We need to live a lifestyle of repentance (see Luke 3:21-22; Matt. 4:17; Acts 2:38; Rev. 3:19).

3. *Communion or friendship with God.* We need to live a lifestyle of intimacy with the Lord (see 2 Cor. 13:14).

4. *Fasting.* We need to emulate Christ's model (see Luke 4:2).

5. *Hearing God.* We need to cultivate the ability to hear the Lord at all times (see John 10:27; 16:13-15; Ps. 32:8).

6. *Obeying the Lord.* We need to live a lifestyle of total obedience (see John 5:19-20; 1 Sam. 15:22).

7. *Exercise our spiritual senses.* We need to live our lives in the Spirit every day (see Heb. 5:14).

8. *Seek the Kingdom of Heaven.* We need to seek the Kingdom of God and His righteousness first (see Matt. 6:33; Luke 12:31; Col. 3:1).

9. *Take the Kingdom of Heaven by force.* At times, we need to seek the Kingdom of God with violence (see Matt. 11:12).

10. *Focus our minds upon Christ and His Kingdom.* We need to focus on the Lord at all times (see Isa. 26:3).

11. *Seek to renew our minds.* We need to earnestly seek to have our mindsets transformed from a carnal

or worldly mindset into a Christ-like or heavenly mindset (see Rom. 12:2).

12. *Invest time studying God's Word.* We need to live a lifestyle of devotion and hide God's Word in our hearts every day (see 2 Tim. 2:15).

13. *Hiddenness.* We need to be open to the Holy Spirit's leading and embrace and obey His leading to enter into a wilderness or hiddenness experience (see Exod. 3:1).

14. *Proclamations.* Begin to speak the promises in God's Word over your life and circumstances (see Job 22:28; Prov. 18:21; Matt. 15:18).

These keys can help you to start the process of rending the heavens over your life. However, you must take the first step. You must purpose in your spirit to seek the Lord with all of your heart. You must follow the example of Christ and practice a lifestyle of prayer and fasting. Don't forget to include daily devotions, separation, consecration, and repentance. Finally, the most basic thing that you can do is to ask the Lord for His will and His plan to open the heavens over your life. Then you will need to be obedient to the Holy Spirit. Let the cry of our hearts be, *"Oh, that You would rend the heavens, and come down!"*

ENDNOTE

1. Strong, James. *Strong's Exhaustive Concordance of the Bible.* Peabody, MA: Hendrickson Publishers, 2007. #G1718.

Chapter 10

ANGELS MANIFEST IN DIVERSE WAYS UNDER OPEN HEAVENS

I t is important that we understand that angels can visit us in various ways. I outlined quite a few methods that angels are revealed to people in my last book. These included some uncommon manifestations such as whirlwinds, balls of lightning, and even balls of fire. Most of these angelic appearances were discerned through the five carnal senses: sight, hearing, smell, taste, and touch. We also looked at the ways that angels manifested to our primary spiritual senses. In summary, I explained to the reader that there were hundreds of ways that God could open up the realm of angels to you. I also encouraged you that it was not necessary to be "fixated" on any one particular manner.[1] In subsequent chapters, I want to elaborate on several additional facets and *modus operandi* that the Lord uses to manifest angelic beings. Not all angelic visits fit into neat little boxes. I believe that we have entered into a season when God will impact ordinary folks by sending angels to invade their dreams.

Many people are beginning to receive revelation about the Kingdom of Heaven when angels break into their dreams. I have been visited in a succession of dreams over the last few years and given a series of revelations. On several occasions I have been visited by the Lord Jesus and by angels in my dreams (see Job 33:15-16). The results of these dreams and visitations have given me sermons, teachings, and prophetic words. You can visit the resource center on our web page to see some of these teachings. The reason I share this is that an angelic encounter that occurs in a dream can be just as real as an "open eye" encounter in the natural and should not be dismissed (see Gen. 28:11-17). Angels are also visiting certain seers to impart revelation. These seers, or what some call "chosen vessels," will not always be well known. Many of God's seers are ordinary men, women, and children.

ANGELS RELEASE GOD'S PRESENCE, ANOINTING, AND GLORY

Some angels spend extended time in the proximity of the Lord around the throne of God. These angels carry the magnified presence and purposes of God into our realm. When they manifest, there is a tangible glory that fills the atmosphere. Often, in such instances, a supernatural spirit of repentance will fall upon a geographic area or group of people as the Lord sovereignly ministers to those present. This dynamic of angelic visitations unfolded in the testimony we saw about the village of Beucelecelli, Tanzania.

An example of this is seen in Isaiah 63:9: *"The Angel of His Presence saved them; in His love and in His pity He redeemed them...."* Another example of an angel that carries this kind of glory is found in Revelation:

After these things I saw another angel coming down from heaven, having great authority, and the earth was illuminated with his glory (Revelation 18:1).

Some angels are anointed to release salvation into the realm of the earth. I call these angels "harvest angels."[2]

We pray for the day to come when the earth is glowing with the glory of God. Let's look at an angelic visitation where this kind of glory manifested over another evangelistic crusade in East Africa. The result of this angelic visitation was the glory of God manifesting, the salvation of thousands, and the release of miracles, signs, and wonders in the heavens above. We are coming into a season when these kinds of "harvester angels" will be seen in every corner of the earth as people preach the Gospel of the Kingdom. The first example of this kind of angelic manifestation of the glory, anointing, and presence of God took place in Tanzania.

PORTAL OVER TANZANIA CRUSADE, 2004

Kathy and I, along with a mission team from the United States, Alaska, and the United Kingdom, were preaching and ministering at the King of Glory Ministry International's first Africa healing crusade. It was "all hallows eve," the high day of occult activity and witchcraft! What a great day to hold a healing crusade in Tanzania! There was a confrontation in the spirit at this crusade. A few local witch doctors opposed the crusade from a high mountain across from the grounds. Heavy, dark clouds pressed in from the west, seemingly to underscore the spiritual confrontation that was occurring in the heavenly realm above the crusade grounds. These ominous black clouds threatened to rain out the crusade. This was exactly what the witch doctors were seeking to accomplish with their spells and incantations. However, God had the victory that day, and His glory was revealed to the people of Tanzania.

When I called for salvation after a message on the Cross and the blood of Jesus, only about 380 of the estimated 3,000 or 4,000 present came to the altar to receive Jesus for the first time. Suddenly, the heavens opened up, and a portal or glory zone manifested over the crusade grounds and the new converts at the altar. I immediately called for the people to look at the sign and wonder that suddenly appeared over them in the open heavens! I told them it was a sign from God, and that God was confirming my words that Jesus is Lord of all. At this same moment, the manifest glory of God and His tangible presence fell upon the people.

Immediately, there were dozens who began to fervently repent! Still others began to violently manifest demons. The glory of God began to flood into the crusade grounds. I told them God was giving them a second chance to repent and receive Jesus as Savior! A spirit of repentance seemed to touch the crowd. The Holy Spirit whispered into my ear, "Pray for salvation a second time." I gave a second invitation for Christ's salvation. We estimate that nearly 3,000 came forward to the altar and prayed to receive Jesus Christ as Savior after the sign in the heavens appeared! *All* glory to God!

ANGELS AFFECT CLIMATE AND ATMOSPHERE

I believe that there are massive angels who have a part to play in co-laboring with people to help give them authority over the weather. These kinds of angelic co-laborers are also responsible for releasing signs and wonders in the heavens, as in the previous testimonies. I call these kinds of angels "signs and wonders" angels. The reason I state this is because of the numerous times that we have seen the weather cooperate with our efforts to hold healing crusades in East Africa's rainy season. In October 2004, the headlines of one local newspaper touted "torrential rains inundate region." The newspaper also had photos of gullies washed away and telephone poles uprooted by the heavy rains. However, we did not have any rain on the grounds where the crusade meetings took place during this same time frame. We only saw the portal of God's glory over the last meeting!

When Kathy and I moved to Tanzania in 2007 to hold seven crusades in seven cities, we experienced a wonderful series of signs and wonders in the heavens above the meetings we organized. In all seven cities, the Lord manifested double rainbows over the altar while we released the message of salvation through Jesus Christ's atoning work. In fact, there were double rainbows over 8 of 33 crusade meetings! Again, we believe that this was due in part to angelic ministry. There was a large angel that manifested in many of those meetings. I believe that he affected the weather in the region near the crusades. I was able to discern this massive harvester angel in each city that we visited that year.

Revelation shows this type of massive angel: *"The angel whom I saw standing on the sea and on the land raised up his hand to heaven"* (Rev. 10:5). There are some massive angels that inhabit the realms of heaven, and at times the Lord sends them into the earth to assist us as we preach the everlasting Gospel of Christ Jesus! I have witnessed huge angels on a handful of occasions, and the next testimony is one such incident.

THE SPIRIT OF GLORY, KANSAS CITY, MAY 2007

There are times when God's angels manifest and bring the tangible glory of our living God with them as they invade our time and space. Kathy and I experienced a powerful visitation of the glory of God in our home in Kansas City in 2007. During that time, I had been fasting and praying, asking the Lord to give more revelation concerning His glory. The Bible is full of accounts of people who have had their lives transformed by experiencing and stepping into the manifest glory of God. Saints like Moses, King David, and Solomon had their destinies and relationships with God accelerated and supernaturally shaped by the glory of God. My desire was to be transformed by the glory of God!

During this season, I had been searching the Scriptures, seeking to dig out the truth in God's Word concerning the *kabod* of God. I looked at the lives of the saints in my exploration for more revelation on the subject. I continued in this quest to encounter God's true glory for several months, from December 2006 right up to October 2007. It seemed to me that the more I sought to understand the glory, the more elusive it seemed to become. I was not interested in what other people said or what books that I read relayed about God's glory. I was on a mission to experience it personally, and I violently pressed into the Lord's Kingdom with prayer and fasting, asking God to introduce me to His glory!

One morning, after I had been reading the Bible and seeking to understand the glory of God, I hit the "wall." I just did not know what to do anymore. It seemed to me that I was no nearer to having an understanding of the glory than I was when I began my studies and investigations months earlier. I fell into bed totally exhausted and more than a little frustrated. I was at the end of my ability and did not know what else to do. I had not touched God's glory in any fashion! I did not have any additional under-standing of the glory of God. In my heart I let out a desperate cry to the Lord saying, "Jesus, I want to know You as the King of Glory. I want to understand the purpose of Your glory. I need

Your help, Lord." And with that I mentally gave up my quest and determined to get some much-needed rest. I looked at the digital clock. It was exactly 4:14 A.M.

I was lying on my stomach, and I had my eyes closed. Suddenly, I could feel flames of glory flashing across my face. There was no possibility of moving my body at all. I was instantly pinned to the bed under the weighty presence of the Lord. Suddenly, fear began to well up within my spirit. Unable to move, I was now a prisoner of the glory! A heavy, weighty, tangible substance began to push down on my body. The more I sought to move, the heavier the weight became and the more alarmed I grew. I was being literally pressed down into the feather top mattress of our bed by the tangible glory of God! For a moment, fear and panic filled my mind. The glory was so intense the thought crossed my mind that I might actually die. With the invasion of God's glory came the reverential fear of the Lord.

I could feel wave after wave of the tangible glory of God flickering over my face and back. This persisted for about two hours nonstop. After about twenty minutes, I was able to hold my fear at bay and decided that I would take a peek to see what was happening. When I opened my, eyes, I saw a blinding pillar of living flames rotating in our bedroom. To my amazement, the pillar of fire reached up and extended through the roof of our bedroom ceiling. It was enormous. This pillar of supernatural fire was spinning in clockwise rotation. It took a few minutes, but my eyes slowly adjusted to see without too much discomfort. Over time, my eyes were fine-tuned to the brightness, and I was able to look at this sign and wonder that had invaded our bedroom. I was mesmerized by what I saw. It occurred to me that I was seeing just a small piece of one leg of a massive angel!

I watched in bewilderment as phosphorescent-colored flames swirled in a clockwise motion and licked my body, buffeting me with heavenly glory. The flames, or arms of glory, were wrapping themselves around my face and back and seemed to caress me. With each passing second, the glory increased. The colors that manifested and spun off of the pillar of ethereal fire were like nothing that I have ever seen before. They were iridescent and shades that I have never seen on earth. Blues, greens, reds, purples, indigos, magnificent yellows, and brilliant golds of indescribable beauty whirled out from the pillar. Each time the arms of iridescent flames of glory washed over me, licking my body, I began to gain more understanding about the glory.

After a time, I began to realize that I was receiving revelation about the glory of God. The Lord was giving me the answer to my prayers. Suddenly, I began to understand how my life had been transformed by the glory of God that had been emitted by Jesus when I had been in His presence. The glory of God had been released within the open heaven that was upon Jesus. It was the glory that was responsible for the grace and favor that came upon saints' lives. It was the glory that gave Solomon the favor and wealth of his life. It was God's glory that released the riches and authority in people's lives. It was the glory of God that the Lord spoke into the hovering of the Holy Spirit and created the heavens and the earth. Humankind was created in God's manifest glory. The glory of God is our inheritance (see Gen. 1)! I also received the revelation during this encounter that the Holy Spirit is the *kabod* glory of God!

Kathy was beside me, semiconscious when this encounter happened, and when she woke up that morning, she, too, had a lot of revelations about the glory of God. As I lay there in the glory, unable to move and unable to sleep, I asked the Lord what I was experiencing. The Holy Spirit told me that I had received the answer to my prayer, and that the spirit of glory had visited me that morning! I thought to myself, "Lord, what in the world is the spirit of glory?" Then I remembered looking at the digital clock when I lay down. It had been exactly 4:14 A.M. Suddenly, I had a "knowing" that the answer to my question was in First Peter 4:14. This Scripture held the key to understanding this pillar of phosphorescent fire that was spinning in our bedroom and appeared to be the leg of a massive angel!

Finally, at about 7:14 A.M., as the sun was starting to rise and the flames from the pillar of fire began to subside and the glory began to lift, I was able to move. After a while I got up and looked at First Peter 4:14 and was astonished to see these words: *"If you are reproached for the name of Christ, blessed are you, for the Spirit of glory and of God rests upon you...."* That was exactly what I had just experienced; the Spirit of God and of glory had "rested" on me!

I read the Scripture and wondered out loud, "Did I just have a visit from the Spirit of glory?" The Holy Spirit spoke to me very clearly that this was the same type of spirit that is found in Hebrews 1:14: *"Are they not all ministering spirits sent forth to minister for those who will inherit salvation?"* The spirit of glory was a ministering spirit! I quickly checked the Greek word in these two passages for "spirit," and the word for spirit used in both passages was *pneuma*. *Pneuma* is translated as, "an angel, God's Spirit, the Spirit of Christ, or the Holy Spirit."[3]

I believe it was an angel that appeared to me in the bedroom! Of course! The spirit of glory ministered to me in the same manner that Hebrews 1:14 describes. I was given revelation and answer to prayer. Ministering to a person is one of the main duties of angels!

I now truly realized that some of God's angelic hosts are truly massive in size! I have occasionally wondered if the huge angel that appeared in our bedroom, the spirit of glory, in some supernatural way played a role in the portal of glory that we saw impact the final day of the crusade later in Mwanza, Tanzania, on October 31, 2007. Hopefully one day I will discover the answer. I had been given so much revelation about the Lord's *kabod* glory that, after church that same afternoon, I came home and wrote four sermons on the glory of God!

For some reason, the Lord seems to enjoy sending angels to our home! Perhaps it is because we invite them, welcome them, and entertain angels in our home. Shortly after we moved into our new home in the mountains of North Carolina, Kathy was witness to an amazing audible manifestation of angelic activity. Again, this angel manifested to one of Kathy's five carnal senses.

SEVEN TRUMPETS SOUND

Here is Kathy's testimony from Saturday, February 7, 2009, at 6:30 A.M.

> The Lord woke me up at 4:30 in the morning, so I went and sat on the sofa in front of the fireplace. He wakes me up almost every morning to be with Him and pray. This particular morning, I felt the joy of the Lord and great happiness to arise and just be with Him. I was smiling from ear to ear. I just sat there with Him and listened, sometimes praying and other times listening. I felt the Holy Spirit and angels in the room, for the air was electric with a lot of angelic activity. All of a sudden, at 6:30, off to my right, I heard a blast of horns. There were seven

horns that sounded extremely loud. The trumpet blasts lasted about seven seconds.

The sound was so loud (like the sound of a train whistle right in the middle of our living room), that my first thought was, *I didn't know there were train tracks near here!* Then I thought, *There aren't any train tracks in Moravian Falls!* It was then that I realized I had heard supernatural horns or trumpets in the spiritual realm. So I asked the Lord what I had heard, and I saw a vision of seven beautiful golden horns or trumpets. Then the Lord told me, "Child, the sounds you hear are the trumpets of Heaven. They are being sounded as a precursor of events that will take place in the earth and above. Listen and obey, for *I am* coming to judge the earth. Things will start to unfold, events so catastrophic as to spark fear in the hearts of My people. Many will turn to Me. Be praying, my child, and watch Me. *Do not take your eyes off Me.* Stay focused, for you shall see the salvation of the Lord unfold in the hearts of My people. Pray, child, pray. Soon, soon."

I believe that the significance of Kathy's encounter with the seven angelic trumpets sounding for seven seconds is very important. The first thing is that the trumpet is a call to war (see 1 Cor. 14:8). I believe that we have entered into the season when the Lord is preparing His Bride for battle, and we must be quick to listen and to obey. Above all, we must pray for God's people and His Church. The second thing that the Lord showed me in relation to this angelic encounter is related to Revelation 8.

When He opened the seventh seal, there was silence in heaven for about half an hour. And I saw the seven angels who stand before God, and to them were given seven trumpets. Then another angel, having a golden censer, came and stood at the altar. He was given much incense, that he should offer it with the prayers of all the saints upon the golden altar which was before the throne. And the smoke of the incense, with the prayers of the saints, ascended before God from the angel's hand. Then the angel took the censer, filled it with fire from the altar, and threw it to the earth. And there were noises, thunderings, lightnings, and an earthquake. So the seven angels who had the seven trumpets prepared themselves to sound (Revelation 8:1-6).

Perhaps Kathy's experience is a sign that the Lord Jesus has begun to hand His seven angels the seven trumpets. That would indicate that we are on the cusp of the days of tribulation. It is also possible that the Lord was giving Kathy a warning and a call to prepare for the coming battle. Of course, this subject matter is the stuff of another book, but it is interesting to note. It might be a good idea to study Revelation 8 at this season. We should also be praying and seeking God for mercy and not judgment at this hour.

FEATHERS FALL

Jesus will surely employ angels in the last days. Perhaps you found these testimonies interesting. As we have traveled throughout the world sharing the Gospel of the Kingdom, we have, from time to time, shared some of the angelic testimonies that are contained in this trilogy. One of the common signs and wonders that often happens when we share about God's angels is that angels' feathers appear and seem to float around Kathy and me as we preach or share our hearts about the angelic realm.

Once, at Christ Triumphant Church in Lee's Summit, Missouri, as I was teaching about the reality of angelic ministry in a King of Glory School of the Supernatural in 2007, the Lord confirmed my preaching about angels with an unusual sign and wonder. Tiny white feathers began to rain down into the service.

My pastor, Alan Koch, started staring at the ceiling of the church as I was preaching about angels. After a few minutes, I stopped and asked him what he was looking at. That is when he told me that feathers were floating around his head and he was looking up to see if he could determine where they were coming from. When he said that, dozens of people who were attending the school also said that they were seeing feathers too. Several of the people had gathered up a few and showed these tiny angels' feathers to me after the session.

Honestly, I don't understand this manifestation of the Kingdom. The feathers are a sign and wonder. I suppose that, as I speak about God's angels, the Lord looses the feathers to confirm my preaching about His angels according to the principle of Mark 16:20: *"They went out and preached everywhere, the Lord working with them and confirming the word through the accompanying signs."* I believe that, at times, the Holy Spirit confirms the messages that we are preaching with the accompanying sign. When I preach about the Cross, God always confirms the message with salvation, miracles, and healings, because that is what the atonement represents.

If you preach prosperity, then God will confirm His Scriptures dealing with God's heart to prosper His people by releasing supernatural prosperity. When you teach on healing, the Lord will confirm your teaching of His Word concerning healing by the Holy Spirit, releasing healing. So sometimes, when I preach or share my heart with folks about the Lord's angelic host and how they occasionally work with me, the Lord will allow tiny brilliant white feathers to rain down around me or anyone who may happen to be nearby! I have also been amazed that others become very angry and irate when you speak about angels' feathers. I have heard it said, "God will offend our mind to test our heart." So I have come to understand that the manifestation of angels' feathers really offends some folks. I don't understand this; but perhaps they just need to "get over it," because if they plan on going to Heaven, I think they will encounter a lot of angels and feathers there, too! I hope that they are not allergic to them!

FEATHERS ANYONE? A TESTIMONY BY JONATHAN AND ROBYN TAN

Once in the United Kingdom, a wonderful couple, Jonathan and Robyn Tan, invited us to dine with them so that we could share more about angels with them in private. Once again, the Lord let it rain feathers.

In 2004, Kevin and Kathy Basconi came to our house for a meal. They were talking about angels, and when we sat down with them after the meal, we noticed tiny feathers appear on Kathy's clothes. It seemed as though an angel was hovering over them. To them it seemed a normal event, but we were completely amazed, and we had a lot of questions about angels and, of course, the feathers.

We couldn't quite believe they were real, and so checked everything I thought had feathers in them—the pillows, jackets, bed covers—but none of the feathers matched at all. It is not that we are cynical; it is just that it seemed too good to be true, really. It was amazing.

Then God seemed to remove any doubt for us on another visit when Kevin came to stay with us. He was again talking about angels. We were sitting opposite him when a feather appeared mid-air—one second it wasn't there, the next it was. We couldn't dispute it. It was a bit larger than the others that we had seen before and was very fine and delicate.

A short time later, Robyn had to collect something from the spare bedroom Kevin was staying in. Just as she walked in the door, a feather appeared mid-air in the middle of the room! She couldn't believe it—two in one day! Although she didn't see an angel with her natural vision, she said she could sense one was in the bedroom there. It seems that when Kevin and Kathy talk about angels, they just show up![4]

So we are beginning to see and understand that there is a strong correlation to open heavens, the ministry of the Holy Spirit, and the release of angelic ministry. At times, when the heavens open, angels will be released through the ministry and unction of the Holy Spirit to manifest Christ's Kingdom upon the earth in various ways. Occasionally, angels will be utilized by God to demonstrate the reality of Christ's Kingdom through signs and wonders. Angels are involved in many different kinds of signs and wonders. In the subsequent chapters, we will begin to investigate some more amazing testimonies of how the Holy Spirit works in symphony with open heavens and angels to manifest signs and wonders upon the earth today.

ENDNOTES

1. See *Dancing With Angels 1*, Chapter 14, "Angels and the Gift of Discerning of Spirits."

2. You may wish to read Dr. R. Edward Miller's inspirational book, *The Secrets of the Argentine Revival.*

3. Strong, James. *Strong's Exhaustive Concordance of the Bible.* Peabody, MA: Hendrickson Publishers, 2007. #G4151.

4. Dr. Jonathan and Robyn Tan, London, England.

Chapter 11

ANGELS AND SIGNS AND WONDERS

Let's continue to elaborate on angels and how they influence signs and wonders. In the last few chapters, we looked at several angelic visitations that ignited or released signs and wonders. I believe that these kinds of angels are being released into many areas of the earth at this hour. It is common to experience these types of angelic encounters in the great harvest fields like Africa, Europe, North America, South America, Asia, the Middle East, and also even in China and the former Soviet Union. Angels like this—angels that can impact the meteorological environment of a region—are what I call "signs and wonders" angels, and they are going to begin to release global revivals and mass salvations through the earth as ordinary people begin to understand how to co-labor with them.

When these angels appear, the atmosphere of the earthly realm is shaken, and supernatural signs appear in the heavens. This sometimes takes the form of an immediate change in the current weather pattern (such as Chinooks).[1] Unusual meteorological phenomenon can happen instantly or can crop up within minutes in association with these angelic visitations. We will begin to witness these signs and wonders angels appear in every corner of the earth as people begin to understand how to co-labor with God's angels. At times, God will release or employ signs and wonders angels to break open the heavens over a region or entire nation.

Things like rain ceasing, torrential rain falling, lone beams of sunshine in overcast skies, rainbows appearing in clear skies, thunder and lightning out of nowhere, glory zones, portals, whirlwinds, violent winds, snowfalls, healing winds, tremors or earthquakes, or what the Scriptures refer to as "wonders in the heavens" sometimes accompany these angels (see Joel 2:30). However, we must also consider that there are circumstances when principalities, powers against the rulers of the darkness of this age, and spiritual hosts of wickedness will at times attempt to influence the weather, and or manifest lying signs and wonders (see Eph. 6:12, and 2 Thess. 2:9). Isn't it wonderful that the Lord has given His friends the delegated power to take authority over these kinds of false phenomenon? That is why we were able to decree peace and take authority over the weather in the name of Jesus Christ in the geographical places where we sought to preach the Gospel of the Kingdom in the midst of demonic opposition. You have this same kind of delegated authority, and when you begin to understand who you are in Christ, you will begin to work the same kinds of sign and wonders that Jesus did and that He has called you to work with your hands and your words (see Mark 4:39).

Often these signs and wonders angels will affect the weather patterns over entire regions. However, sometimes the effects are limited to a small area. These signs and wonders angels affect the spiritual atmosphere over regions too. They carry an ability to break open the heavens, activating the release of biblical miracles, healings, signs and wonders, and wholesale salvation. This can occur over an individual, city, region, nation, or even an entire continent. It was angels like these that helped initiate the Argentine Revival by co-laboring with men like Dr. Edward R. Miller, and then later others like Omar Cabrera, Carlos Annacondia, Hector Gimenez, and Claudio Freidzon.

On occasion, I have actually seen angels manifest when these signs and wonders in the heavens have transpired. After much prayer and study of the Scriptures, I believe that there is evidence of this in the Bible. Joel 2:30 clearly tells us that God will reveal Himself in the last days in this manner (wonders in the heavens). Look at this passage:

> *And it shall come to pass afterward that I will pour out My Spirit on all flesh; your sons and your daughters shall prophesy, your old men shall dream dreams, your young men shall see visions. And also on My menservants and on My maidservants I will pour out My Spirit in those days. And I will show wonders in the heavens and in the earth: blood and fire and pillars of smoke. The sun shall be turned into darkness, and the moon into blood, before the coming of the great and awesome day of the LORD. And it shall come to pass that whoever calls on the name of the LORD shall be saved. For in Mount Zion and in Jerusalem there shall be deliverance, as the LORD has said, among the remnant whom the LORD calls* (Joel 2:28-32).

This passage clearly promotes God's intentions to release signs and wonders in our time. Many times the Lord employs angels to manifest these signs in the heavens above.

A Season of Signs and Wonders

In the fall of 2007, Kathy and I preached in seven miracle crusades in seven cities in northwest Tanzania. These meetings took place between October 17 and December 9, 2007. This is considered the rainy season in Tanzania. During the rainy season, it rains every day and has for eons in East Africa. You can set your watch by the afternoon and evening rains during the rainy season. However, in the 33 crusade meetings we conducted in those seven cities, it only rained on the crusade meetings two times (in one city), and those two bursts of rain came after the Gospel had been preached. In addition to this, the Lord gave us wonderful signs and wonders in the heavens in all seven cities. We saw double rainbows develop over the altar eight days during the 33 crusade meetings. That is nearly 25 percent of the time. That is not a coincidence. Neither is it a coincidence that 95 percent of the crusade meetings held in the rainy season were clear and dry. God confirms the preaching of His Word with signs and wonders in the heavens above. The Lord often employs angels to help accomplish this task.

Often, when you travel into a nation and begin to declare the Gospel of the Kingdom in a city that is under the sway of the god of this world, there is a great battle in the heavens above that region (see 1 John 5:19). Remember that Jesus Himself prophesied that:

> *This gospel of the kingdom will be preached in all the world as a witness to all the nations, and then the end will come* (Matthew 24:14).

When we are actively seeking to further God's Kingdom by the preaching of the Gospel of His Kingdom, the enemy is actively seeking to hinder Christ's Gospel. Hence we are given the term "spiritual warfare." Signs and wonders angels are activated in these kinds of circumstances. As the result of angelic activities in the heavenly realms, signs in the heavens above often materialize in these situations. Many times signs and wonders result because of spiritual warfare in heavens over a geographic area where the Gospel is being released.

As we pour out our lives as a drink offering, preaching the Gospel of His Kingdom, the Lord will release and empower angelic ministry to assist us. We see an example of this kind of sign and wonder angel, or harvest angel, in Revelation 18:1: *"After these things I saw another angel coming down from heaven, having great authority, and the earth was illuminated with his glory."* There is also this very clear description of the effects of the visitation of a signs and wonders angel at the resurrection of Jesus Christ:

> *And behold, there was a great earthquake; for an angel of the Lord descended from heaven, and came and rolled back the stone from the door, and sat on it. His countenance was like lightning, and his clothing as white as snow. And the guards shook for fear of him, and became like dead men. But the angel answered and said to the women, "Do not be afraid, for I know that you seek Jesus who was crucified"* (Matthew 28:2-5).

Therefore, there is certainly scriptural evidence to support this kind of angelic activity and ministry today. Sometimes when these signs and wonders angels show up, the earth still quakes!

There have been dozens of times when we have seen the angels of God manifest in our soul-winning outreaches and release glory zones, portals, open heavens, or signs and wonders in our midst. These signs and wonders have been common in our ministry as we have ministered in Africa, Europe, the United States, and beyond. These types of supernatural occurrences and associated angelic activity will become much more common in the approaching season. We will begin to see God's people empowered to co-labor with His angelic host to impact the earth for Christ's glory to manifest the reality of His Kingdom in the middle of hardhearted and unbelieving nations. All of these signs and wonders will point people to Jesus as the Messiah.

On all of the occasions mentioned above, I discerned a large angel descending from the realms of Heaven onto the crusade grounds or places that we were preaching about the Gospel of the Kingdom. I am certain that the angel's manifestation disturbed the meteorological environment and atmosphere over these areas. The signs in the heavens above were an indication of the angel's presence. The glory of God was also manifest and certainly played a role in the multiplication of the number of souls that were saved in these instances.

The Lord is accelerating this kind of angelic ministry at this hour. Many evangelists who preach the true Gospel—the Gospel of His Kingdom—will actually have encounters with these mighty harvester angels, and you can too. That is the hour that we are living in at this time, and God has ordained for you to be a part of the greatest outpouring of His Spirit the world has ever seen. What a time to be alive!

Revelation details these characteristics of angels like this.

Then the angel took the censer, filled it with fire from the altar, and threw it to the earth. And there were noises, thunderings, lightnings, and an earthquake (Revelation 8:5).

The birth of Christ was also accompanied by angelic visitations and signs in the heavens above (see Matt. 2). These supernatural encounters should not be so unbelievable to us. Jesus is an awesome God, and He is able to release dramatic demonstrations of His Kingdom and Lordship as He wills. The previous testimonies from Beucelecelli, Kansas City, and Mwanza illustrate this unfolding dynamic of this type of angelic ministry. In the next chapter, I want to share another powerful testimony of a similar appearance of such a signs and wonders angel that occurred in 2005 that was life changing for many people who were involved.

ENDNOTE

1. *Chinooks* are warming winds that come down from the mountains or in from the sea and change the climate in an area very quickly.

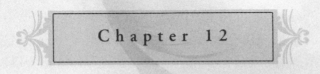

Chapter 12

THE HOLY SPIRIT AND SIGNS AND WONDERS ANGELS

THE NETHERLANDS, 2005

Sometimes I wonder why we see some of the signs and wonders and angels that the Lord releases as we minister. We are not sure why these supernatural things occur for the most part. However, on one occasion we did find out one reason for a very unusual sign and wonder some two years later. We had been invited to minister in the city of Hoogeveen in the Netherlands by Maurits and Esther Tuinenburg of Tabernacle Ministries. They were holding a miracles, signs, and wonders conference in the city. We were asked to minister in healing, and they were hoping that God would open up the region to miracles and healings. A prominent healing evangelist from the Netherlands, Jaap Dieleman, was also scheduled to preach and minister. We had been praying and asking our intercessors from the King of Glory Prayer Shield to pray for "unusual signs and wonders."

However, what transpired the very first morning of the conference was mind-blowing! Our guests had asked Jaap to conduct the miracle service scheduled for the first night, and I had been wrestling with the Lord for a direction for the ministry. I was to speak first at the conference and set the tone for the meetings that were starting the next morning. As I prayed, the Lord spoke to me and instructed me to read from Luke 3:22 to start the conference. As I studied this chapter of Luke, it seemed very appropriate for a miracles, signs, and wonders conference. Honestly, I was not sure that we were going to see a lot of signs and wonders.

The Netherlands can be extremely hard to minister in, and the conference was being held in a denominational church building that did not believe in the gifts of the Spirit, much less signs and wonders. The sanctuary was beautiful and was constructed of very old stone-carved walls. The building had been constructed several hundred years ago. There were beautiful stained-glass windows on the sides of the edifice. These windows were very large, perhaps 45 feet in height and about 18 feet wide. They had wonderful blue stained-glass murals in each panel, and there were stained-glass panels on both sides of the sanctuary.

The first session was to begin bright and early at 10:00 A.M. It was a great day full of fresh air and sunshine. My heart was pregnant with possibilities, but it seemed that the sanctuary was full of unbelief. I was ready to go and was feeling a somewhat uneasy anticipation in my spirit when I stepped up to the podium. I could sense that many of the hundred or so people had come the conference with an attitude of, "I will believe it (miracles, signs, and wonders) when I see it." I told the people to turn to Luke 3. I was admiring the beauty of the tall stained-glass window to my left on the platform as I laid my Bible down on the podium. Amazingly, my trusty Bible opened to Luke 3 on its own, just like it had done before in Daisy's little cabin. I smiled. The early morning sunshine was streaming through the tall stained-glass windows on the left side of the sanctuary and giving the room a wonderful supernatural feel. *This is nice,* I thought.

I took a deep breath and said to those in attendance, "Let's start in verse 22." As I said that, I noticed that Kathy was looking at the stained-glass with great trepidation. I read these words:

And the Holy Spirit descended in bodily form like a dove upon Him, and a voice came from heaven which said, "You are My beloved Son; in You I am well pleased" (Luke 3:22).

As I said this last phrase, I *felt* a shadow as it blotted out the sun that was filtering in through the blue window to my left. I turned to see a shadow of a bird that was flying directly at the window. I could see the dark outline of the bird very well and could recognize that the bird was just about to hit the window. Before I could think or say anything, the shadow did make contact with the stained-glass window, and to my amazement, the bird erupted through the stained glass! I was astonished because the beautiful stained glass window was not broken. Rather the dove had supernaturally passed through the material of the stained glass in the same way that I have seen angels walk through solid doors to enter rooms!

I stood in stunned silence for about thirty seconds as the most beautiful, iridescent white dove that I had ever seen materialized inside of the sanctuary. At that precise instant the heavens opened, and it seemed that when the dove exploded through the glass, there was an immediate release of God's glory upon this dove's arrival.

It seemed that the Holy Spirit had indeed descended in the bodily form of a beautiful dove into the sanctuary. I looked at the Holy Spirit or dove. It was the most enchanting dove that I have ever seen. For about ten seconds, the dove hovered in one spot just in front of the window in the bright sunshine. It was about thirty feet from my head, and I could see it in great detail. The feathers of its wings seemed to be phosphorescent. They emitted a sort of sky-blue glow, but there were a myriad of other colors within the wing feathers as well. The halo of colors seemed to explode from the wings in all directions as the dove hovered in place, flapping its wings. We had been given our first sign and wonder!

These colors were stunning. However, the most remarkable thing that was instantly discernible to almost everyone was the manifest glory of God that filled the sanctuary. I turned to my left to gaze at this incredible sign and wonder, and the holy dove hovered and seemed to look around the sanctuary for a place to come to rest. It seemed that a phosphorescent corona or halo was being emitted by our supernatural visitor. Honestly, I am not able to adequately describe the appearance and glory of this dove. The other thing that I was also immediately aware of was the presence of angels. Lots of angels had suddenly joined the miracles, signs, and wonders conference. The fragrance of frankincense and myrrh permeated the air, my left hand went numb, and almost every hair on my body stood on end! The holy dove hovered for another five seconds, and then it took off like a shot and flew right at my head. It swooped down, and I saw it very clearly as it flew past me and I spun around to see the dove fly into the far back corner of the platform, and with a flash it disappeared! I stared at the spot in disbelief for a moment. I had forgotten where I was and what I was doing! I was lost in the glory of God. All of this transpired in less than a minute.

A second later, I remembered and turned back to the congregation and was amazed to see many of them staring at the spot where the dove had just flown to and vanished into thin air. Their mouths were hanging open! I screamed, "How many of you saw that?" Several hands shot up! I said, "The power of God is here to heal." I knew this because the Lord had told me in prayer that when I felt the angel near to call for the deaf and the Lord would heal them. Since my arm and hand were numb and my hair was standing on end, I knew this was the time. I said, "There are two women here, one is totally deaf and one is deaf in one ear. You have been praying and asking God for your miracle. Come to the altar now and Jesus will heal you!"

Immediately, two women of African descent came to the altar. Kathy and I quickly prayed for them both, and Jesus healed both of them by the first prayer. One woman had been deaf in one ear for 37 years, and the other had been deaf from birth—47 years. They were both instantly healed in the presence and glory of God within the open heaven. They both began to weep violently. I asked them to share their testimonies. We did this in order to help build the faith of the other people in attendance. Both women were from Guyana, South America. The first one testified through tears that she had brought her deaf friend to the miracles, signs, and wonders conference after she saw an advertisement for the meetings.

She prayed and felt that the Lord told her that if she went, He would heal her ear. She raised one hand in the air and began to jump up and down and weep massively, shouting, "I am healed! I can hear, I can hear, praise Jesus, I can hear; my deaf ear is healed!" The woman went on in this fashion for about five minutes, and then we finally got her friend's testimony. She was also totally healed and was also crying to the extent that she was unable to speak. However, with the help of her friend, we did succeed in confirming that the Lord had healed her deaf ears as well. Since she had never heard at all, she could not speak very well. Clearly, the two had always communicated via sign language.

Since she was weeping uncontrollably, it was nearly impossible to get her story from her, but her friend seemed to be able to understand her through the tears of joy. At that point, we just opened up the meeting and began to minister in the word of knowledge, which was activated and in operation as the tangible presence of the Holy Spirit hung in our midst. Again, it appeared that the Holy Spirit was working in harmony or symphony with the angelic realm and open heavens to release the gifts of the Spirit in our midst. Many others were healed and set free that morning. However, the most amazing thing was the appearance of the Holy Spirit in the form of that phosphorescent dove. I wondered about that surreal supernatural sign and wonder for a long time. Surely the Lord had a plan and a purpose for the dove manifesting into our meeting in that fashion.

BAS DE ROOS' TESTIMONY

When Kevin and Kathy Basconi visited us in Hoogeveen, during the first meeting Kevin was just preparing to preach. Suddenly, I noticed a bird, a dove, flying outside the church. This dove was flying toward a very large church window. It looked like the dove was going to hit the window, but somehow it seemed to fly through the window. At that time, I was very focused on Kevin preaching, and I did not think too much about the bird. But then Kevin said that he also saw the Holy Spirit descend as a dove into the meeting.

Then I understood that what I had seen was in the spirit and not in the natural. Several other people, including my wife, Klarimske, also saw the dove coming into the church and exploding into the building with a burst of colors. I believe that this was a sign of the heavens that opened, because in the same meeting there were a lot healings and miracles. I also remember something about two deaf people who were healed in that meeting. I think one was an older woman, and the other was of African descent and was dark-skinned.[1]

MAURITS' TESTIMONY

During the first session of a signs and wonders conference we did in Hoogeveen, I was just relaxing after I did worship, hanging out on the right side of the building together with my wife and our firstborn child, Sammy. I was a little tired and also was holding our baby, so I didn't fully follow what was being said by Kevin when he started speaking. However, at a certain point during his speaking, I suddenly noticed the shadow of a dove very clearly coming down and then flying through the light that a projector was still projecting on the projection screen. So then I saw the shadow of the bird on the screen for a few seconds while he went over the projection screen and then suddenly disappeared. I tried to find the bird but without success. Only thing that I remember is that after that the air was filled with anticipation and healings started to occur. Several deaf ears were opened—one lady in particular who was born deaf and another lady who had been deaf for over 30 years! Several others came forward and received healing for different conditions. It was an awesome weekend we will always remember.[2]

KATHY'S TESTIMONY

It was a beautiful sunny day. I was sitting in the front pew of the church, and Kevin was speaking about different things before he was going to preach. When he was ready to preach, he told us to open our Bibles to the Book of Luke chapter 3, and he had just started reading. For some reason, I started to stare at one of the stained-glass windows in the church near the right side of the altar. The sun was shining through them, and they were very beautiful at that moment. All of a sudden, I saw the shadow of a bird in the distance. It appeared to be flying in the direction of the stained-glass windows. I watched as the shadow of the bird got bigger and bigger and bigger. The thought came to me that the bird was going to collide with the stained-glass window. So I said, "Lord, help that bird; please don't let it hit the window." All of a sudden, the shadow got very big, and to my amazement the bird flew through the window!

When the bird came through, there was an explosion of power and also an eruption of colors that seemed to be super white. I was surprised to see the bird was a beautiful white dove. After it came through the window, it stayed in midair for a few seconds. As its wings were fluttering, I saw beautiful royal blues between the dove's pin feathers. The color blue was like no other color blue that I have ever seen on earth before. I watched in amazement, and the bird sort of illuminated the area in front of the stained-glass window. It was a supernatural phenomenon the way the dove hovered in the bright morning sunshine. The brilliant blue stained-glass windows served as a perfect backdrop for the shimmering blues that seemed to emanate from the dove's wings. I have never seen colors so beautiful in my life. Then the dove took off at light speed, flying in Kevin's direction, and flew behind him to the sanctuary's vaulted ceiling and just disappeared in a flash.

I looked around the sanctuary to see if I could find where the bird had flown to. It had just totally disappeared. It was gone! Then Kevin asked, "Did any of you just see that?" As Kevin asked the question, I realized that what I had seen was the Holy Spirit coming in the form of a dove. I was totally awed by the experience. The presence of the Holy Spirit was tangible, and I could really feel the love of God. But really it was just utter joy that the Holy Spirit had come into conference. It was just so beautiful and holy to actually see the person of the Holy Spirit with my own eyes. There were also very powerful healings that happened that morning. I remember two deaf women being healed and many other healings too. There were several others who also saw the dove fly into the meeting through the window. What an awesome sight to behold!

A WOMAN'S TESTIMONY

In 2007, our friends from Tabernacle Ministries invited Kathy and me to return to the city of Gorredijk to minister in a school of the supernatural. One evening, I was sharing the testimony about

the Holy Spirit attending the miracles, signs, and wonders conference in the form of a dove. I shared in great detail the whole testimony, and I was just about to move on to another topic when the
Holy Spirit nudged me to ask if anyone present now in Gorredijk
had been in that meeting two years earlier in Hoogeveen. When
I asked, a woman immediately jumped up with a big smile on her
face and said, "It is true. I was in that meeting, and a dove did fly
through the stained-glass window! I saw everything!"

I could see that she was very excited about the fact that I had
shared about the event, and I asked her if she might like to give her
testimony about exactly what she saw. She was very happy to come
and share her experience with the group of about 40 people. As it
turned out, her testimony ministered more to me than I was able
to minister to the people on that day! Here is what she said, to the
best of my memory and limited notes from the meetings:

> Yes, I was in Hoogeveen that morning. I had told God
> that I was really through. I had been struggling with my
> faith for a long time. My son was a drug addict, and
> he was involved in terrible things. I told God, "This is
> Your last chance with me. I am going to this supposed
> 'miracles, signs, and wonders conference,' and if You do
> not give me a sign then I am going to go back into the
> world and forget all about Jesus and God."
>
> It sounds very hard now, but at that time I was just at the
> end of my mind and was really desperate. Well, before
> you started to preach, you were talking about your CDs
> and teachings, and you asked if anyone had a son who
> was addicted to drugs. I held my hand up and you gave
> me the CD about your testimony called "From the

Gutter to Glory." As you handed it to me, you smiled at me and said, "Please give this to you son. We have seen a lot of people saved when they hear my testimony. It is full of the supernatural. You may not be able to get him to attend church, but he may listen to this stuff about angels, miracles, and stuff." You were just about to walk away, and then you turned back to me and said, "God really is going to use this to touch your son. He will be saved and delivered within one year." Well, I just did not know what to think, but in my heart there was a spark of hope. You had such a gentle manner and such a genuine firmness when you told me that my son would be saved.

Well, I was thinking about all that you had said when I realized that you had told everyone to open their Bibles. I looked up from my Bible, and I saw you turn your head quickly to the left and look at the big window there. The sun was shining through the window, and the second I looked at the window I saw the dove that you talked about come through the glass! It was amazing! I saw it with my own eyes, and it seemed to glow. For just a moment it just seemed to float in that spot in front of the window. It was mesmerizing. It was obvious to me that this dove was not of this world. Suddenly, the dove flew behind your head, and I watched it as it sort of disappeared in the other side of the church. Then I heard God! God spoke to me very clearly and said, "Are you still going to leave Me?" I knew that the Lord had answered my prayer. God had given me a sign. I began to cry, and a great peace and happiness came into my heart.

I just knew that my son would be saved. I just had faith for some reason.

When I got home, it was a few days before I saw my son again, but I told him about you and gave him the CD. He told me he did not want to listen to it, but I noticed that he did take it about three days later. He later told me that he would start to listen to it and cut it off, but finally he listened to the whole thing, and at the end when you pray for salvation and deliverance, he prayed too. He did ask Jesus to come to be his Savior, and he was also freed from the heroin almost in one day or so. Now he in studying in a Bible school, and he is soon to graduate. He wants to be a youth pastor. That day God used that dove to change my life, and also the life of my son.

ANGELS IN THE LAST DAYS

I am certain that angels are available to help those who are preaching God's Word in the great last days' harvest. It is possible that many evangelists and ministers can and will encounter these kinds of signs and wonders angels in the coming days. In reference to our examination of angelic beings, I am not suggesting that everyone who is reading this will experience these kinds of supernatural experiences and angelic visitations, but with God nothing is impossible! However, I want to document them because they are a reality. Signs and wonders angels and harvester angels are very real. Certainly the Lord will release more and more of these kinds of angelic beings as we approach the second coming of Jesus.

These kinds of angels have been associated with the release and sparking of the great revivals in church history. We have included these examples and testimonies of signs and wonders angels to encourage you, to challenge you, and to stir you up to press into the Word of God for yourself. These signs and wonders angels will not only be involved in revival and harvest, but they will also have an important role to play in the great tribulation. You may wish to study Revelation 6, as we may be living on the cusp of the hour of Revelation 6. If this is true, then you may wish to consider the signs and wonders angels that are seen in Revelation 7 through 12. I suggest this Scripture study to you for your edification.

Of course, not every visitation of the Holy Spirit is going to be this dynamic, mystical, or supernatural in nature. This was a very special kiss from the Lord. He truly loves His people and at times manifests His Kingdom for all to see just like we studied earlier in Luke 3, Matthew 17, and Acts 1. In fact, Jesus promised that people would see God manifest in our time. I do not want you to take my word for this fact; look at the words of Christ:

He who has My commandments and keeps them, it is he who loves Me. And he who loves Me will be loved by My Father, and I will love him and manifest Myself to him (John 14:21).

The word Jesus used in this passage for "manifest" is the Greek word *emphanizō. Emphanizō* can be translated as "to exhibit (in person), such as a fine masterpiece or painting in a museum, or to disclose by appearance, to show something plainly."[3] That is exactly what the Holy Spirit did in Hoogeveen.

As I have remunerated and pondered this fascinating experience in my heart over the years, I believe that the Lord has given me some additional insights and revelation about what we witnessed in Hoogeveen that sunny morn. When the Holy Spirit manifests upon the earth, angels are often released and accompany the third part of the God-head into our realm through an open heaven. Perhaps, when the Holy Spirit fell in Acts 2, He was also accompanied by numerous angelic beings. Let's examine this possibility for a moment. Look at Acts 2:

> *When the Day of Pentecost had fully come, they were all with one accord in one place. And suddenly there came a sound from heaven, as of a rushing mighty wind, and it filled the whole house where they were sitting. Then there appeared to them divided tongues, as of fire, and one sat upon each of them. And they were all filled with the Holy Spirit and began to speak with other tongues, as the Spirit gave them utterance* (Acts 2:1-4).

When the Holy Spirit fell in power on the Day of Pentecost, we are given a detailed description of the event. We are told that they saw *"divided tongues, as of fire* (possibly an angel or angels), *and one sat upon each of them."* From this description, it would seem that all of the 120 in the upper room were touched by separate tongues of fire, and as they were touched by the tongues of fire, they were all filled with the Holy Spirit and spoke in a heavenly language. The Scriptures do not spell this out clearly, but perhaps there were 120 individual tongues of fire and each one touched a separate individual in the room. Remember what we have learned from Hebrews: *"Of the angels He says: 'Who makes His **angels** spirits and His ministers a **flame of fire'"** (Heb. 1:7 emphasis mine).

I believe what actually occurred on the day of Pentecost was a rending or opening of the heavens and a visitation of the Holy Spirit. The Holy Spirit was accompanied by a small regiment of angels, 120 or so, that manifested as flames of fire. Of course, this is somewhat extra-biblical, and you should pray and search the Scriptures concerning this matter for yourself. Personally, I have never heard this idea or theology preached or spoken of before, though it must have been preached by someone. What if those divided tongues of fire were angels? That would surely indicate that the Lord is still using His angels to implement His plans concerning the Church. This idea was something that I have never fathomed or heard propagated at all in the past.

One last point needs to be made here. On the morning of February 4, 2010, at 5:56 A.M., I was visited in my dreams by an angel. This was the third angel that Jesus had assigned to me in the realm of Heaven that I documented in my previous book. In this dream, this scribe angel handed me a copy of the book that you are now holding in your hands. In fact, at that time the manuscript was not finalized, nor was the book published! The angel opened the new book and pointed to this chapter with his right index finger and said, "Read here." In the dream or vision, I read the ending for this chapter. The scribe angel smiled at me and handed me the book, carefully keeping the place that he wanted me to read open with the thumb of his right hand. I looked into his piercing blue eyes and smiled back. There was a great peace that emanated from my friend and co-worker. I took the book gently from his hands and placed my thumb in the place he had indicated, but I turned the book over to look at the cover. I was also very pleased with the art work for the cover of this new book and smiled greatly. The angel continued to smile at me and appeared to be quite pleased as well. I could feel the weight of the book in my hands and could see the colors of the design. I was quite pleased with the finished product.

What I read in the book was the last four paragraphs that precede this sentence. So the revelation about the tongues of fire described in Acts 2 on the day of Pentecost actually being a manifestation of angelic beings was given to me by a scribe angel in a "God dream" or a vision! Again, at times angels visit us in dreams, and these visitations should not be ignored!

I want to encourage you to be cognizant in the presence of the Holy Spirit, because as the Holy Spirit begins to manifest, there are frequently hosts of angels present as He comes. In these instances, we have great opportunity to exercise our spiritual senses and then recognize the angels that are present. We should also keep an open mind and remember that God's angels can appear in many different ways. Encountering angels and signs and wonders should just be a normal part of your walk with Jesus. And they should be only one small tool or weapon of spiritual warfare that is at your disposal to manifest Christ's Kingdom according to the will of the Lord. What an awesome God!

In the next chapter, I want to share about the role of the priesthood of all believers and the part God's royal priesthood will play in the approaching global revivals and outpourings of the Holy Spirit.[4] It is important that we understand that we *are* a royal priesthood and that God has a very special calling and purpose for each of us. In the next chapter, we will examine the priesthood of all believers from Christ's perspective and from the example that the Messiah left for you and me.

ENDNOTES

1. Bas de Roos, Software Engineer.
2. Maurits Tuinenburg, Tabernacle Ministries.

3. Strong, James. *Strong's Exhaustive Concordance of the Bible*. Peabody, MA: Hendrickson Publishers, 2007. #G1718.

4. I touched on this concept briefly in *Dancing With Angels 1*. However, I did not elaborate on this powerful transformation that is coming to God's people.

Chapter 13

PREPARING YOUR HEART AS THE PRIESTHOOD OF ALL BELIEVERS

We are living in the hour when the priesthood of all believers will come into fruition. We can access the realms of Heaven and decree the things that we both see and hear in the heavenly places. Of course, this has been a primary theme of this book and *Dancing With Angels 1*. I have shared with the reader and encouraged you that we have stepped into the hour and day when "any ol' whosoever" can have these same kinds of supernatural encounters and interact with angels and enter into the open heavens. Once we begin to co-labor with angels, we will be able to impact our spheres of influence and geographical areas by releasing the Kingdom of Heaven on earth (see Rev. 19:10; 22:9). Again, this dynamic is only possible because of the finished work of Christ and the authority that He has given to you and me (see Matt. 9:8; 28:18).

The apostle Peter illustrated this mandate and Kingdom principle in First Peter:

You are a chosen generation, a royal priesthood, a holy nation, His own special people, that you may proclaim the praises of Him who called you out of darkness into His marvelous light; who once were not a people but are now the people of God, who had not obtained mercy but now have obtained mercy (1 Peter 2:9-10).

The Lord has called you and me to be royal priests of heavenly light or heavenly revelation. We are called to be people of God or people *with* God. We need to learn to walk in this calling and authority. God's people have been given the right and privilege to walk in the heavenly places. We have been created in the very image of God to be priests after the order of Melchizedek. We were created to be priests after the exact image of Christ Jesus. To accomplish this mandate, we must enter into the heavenly realms through the open heavens and obtain supernatural revelations, wisdom, and plans directly from God just like Jesus did.

THE ORDER OF MELCHIZEDEK

Melchizedek was a priest of great significance and importance. He was considered to be the king of peace or the king of righteousness. These are both foreshadows of the Messiah. In fact, many theologians believe that the appearance of Melchizedek was a theophany or pre-incarnate visitation of Jesus in the life of Abraham. Genesis describes this role: *"Melchizedek king of Salem brought out bread and wine; he was the priest of God Most High"* (Gen. 14:18). We are also called to be priests of the Most High God. Bread and wine are a foreshadowing of the Lord's Supper or the communion table, and these speak of both friendship and intimacy with God. We also see that the psalmist describes the role of Christ as a priest after the order of Melchizedek. *"The Lord has sworn and will not relent, 'You are a priest forever according to the order of Melchizedek'"* (Ps. 110:4). This last Scripture also applies personally—you are also called to be a priest forever according to the order of Melchizedek.

Therefore, it is important that we have an understanding of the role of the Melchizedek priesthood. We find more revelation about Melchizedek from the author of Hebrews:

> *For He testifies: "You are a priest forever according to the order of Melchizedek." For on the one hand there is an annulling of the former commandment because of its weakness and unprofitableness, for the law made nothing perfect; on the other hand, there is the bringing in of a better hope, through which we draw near to God. And inasmuch as He was not made priest without an oath (for they have become priests without an oath, but He with an oath by Him who said to Him: "The Lord has sworn and will not relent, 'You are a priest forever according to the order of Melchizedek'")* (Hebrews 7:17-21).

Christ came and gave us a better covenant. It was only through the cleansing blood, forgiveness, and salvation of Christ's work of Calvary that humankind could begin to have our conscience cleansed from sin, transgression, and iniquity to *boldly* come into God's Presence. Christ opened the heavens for us and made a way for humankind to be cleansed, allowing us to be reunited with the Father and the Holy Spirit so that we can boldly come before the throne of grace in the heavenly or spiritual realms.

As we have previously stated, the Lord came to give us a model to emulate, and He broke open the heavens for you and me, giving us free access into the heavenly realms. So we need to understand that we are also called to be priests after the model of Melchizedek who was both priest and king. We are called to the fullness of the Melchizedek priesthood. That is what you are called to be—a royal or kingly priest. Just as Christ's role as our High Priest is to pass into the heavens, so are we all called to also ascend, and descend into, from the heavens. Just as Christ is called to be our eternal priest, we are also called to be eternal priests forever around the throne of God with Kingdom—or kingly (Christ's)—authority (see Rev. 5:11; 7:11-12).

Melchizedek's royal priesthood is a parabolic shadow of Christ's role as both King and Priest. Christ also ministered in the role or office of the apostle and prophet (as well as the other ministry offices found in Ephesians 4—teacher, evangelist, pastor). We need to understand the fullness of each of these roles of the priesthood after the order of Melchizedek. Christ is calling ordinary folks to operate in a similar fashion and in the very same Kingdom authority today. The priesthood after the order of Melchizedek is superior to the Levitical priesthood established by the Law of Moses. The Levitical priesthood was based upon genealogy and not a blood oath. It was limited to one tribe of Israel, the Levites. The priesthood that is established according to the order of Melchizedek is an eternal priesthood and is based upon a better covenant. Christ's covenant is based upon His blood and the atonement of Calvary. Our oath is also based on our acceptance, confession, and belief in the power of the blood of Christ that makes you and me royal priests after the order of Melchizedek. Hebrews makes this fact clear: *"By so much more Jesus has become a surety of a better covenant"* (Heb. 7:22). In other words, Jesus guarantees you and me a better covenant and priesthood than the covenant of Moses and the Levitical priesthood. Based upon Christ's own blood, we have a better covenant and a superior blood oath as a royal priesthood.

We see a wonderful description of Christ's priestly duties as a Priest after the order of Melchizedek in Hebrews:

> *Seeing then that we have a great High Priest who has passed through the heavens, Jesus the Son of God, let us hold fast our confession. For we do not have a High Priest who cannot sympathize with our weaknesses, but was in all points tempted as we are, yet without sin. Let us therefore come boldly to the throne of grace, that we may obtain mercy and find grace to help in time of need* (Hebrews 4:14-16).

Christ, through His finished work and sinless life, has passed through and into the heavenly realms, and He has given you and me the same privileges, too. Remember, opening the heavens over humankind was one of Christ's primary missions. He accomplished this by defeating the enemy with His shed blood and death on the Cross.

Jesus has given us an example to follow, and we can have free access to also pass into the heavenly realms and come directly to the throne of God with our requests and prayers. As a kingly Priest, Christ has the liberty to enter into the heavenly realms and make His requests directly to the Father. We have also been given this privilege and authority through Christ's work of atonement. We no longer need a Levitical priest to mediate for us with God. Christ did that once and for all on the Cross and gave us free access to God our Father through the open heavens.

As royal priests after the order of Melchizedek, we are called to be priests of a higher order than the Old Testament model of the priests of Levi. We see this dynamic illustrated in Hebrews:

> *Therefore, if perfection were through the Levitical priest-hood (for under it the people received the law), what further need was there that another priest should rise according to the order of Melchizedek, and not be called according to the order of Aaron?* (Hebrews 7:11)

We are called to be priests after the model of Jesus, a royal or kingly priesthood. This is possible because Christ has opened the heavens for us. Jesus has made a way for you and me to access the heavenly realms through open heavens and come boldly to the throne of grace. We are living in the day and hour that the Lord is anointing ordinary people's eyes with eye salve in order that we can see His Kingdom and release it upon the earth. Christ has counseled us to purchase eye salve and to see and hear from the heavenly realms. Once we begin to grasp this dynamic and set it in motion in our lives, we will, at times, see the angels that are busily working on God's behalf. At other times, we will be empowered by the unction of the Holy Spirit to co-labor with God's angels.

However, this is a learning process. We need to have our minds renewed and our mindsets challenged and changed. We need to have the understanding that this kind of eternal and heavenly ministry is possible for you and me today. Often it takes a period of time to comprehend and come to this realization and revela-tion. However, when our minds are renewed and realigned with the plans and purposes of Heaven, we will realize how easy it is to release the Kingdom of Heaven upon the earth in the same way that Jesus did. We will ascend vertically into the heavens to gain revelation knowledge. Then we will release or decree that revelatory knowledge horizontally upon the earth to loose the Kingdom of Heaven. This is actually a picture of the Cross and the model of prayer that Christ taught His royal priesthood to emulate (see Matt. 6:10; Luke 11:2). This model of ministry is illustrated in many of the supernatural testimonies found in this trilogy.

That is the reason that many in the Body of Christ are being purged during this season. Of course, Christ Jesus purged our sins with His atoning work on the Tree of Calvary. However, we must also submit to the Lord's refining process to become God's friends. We must allow the Holy Spirit to renew our minds, and we must have our thoughts transformed into the mind of Christ. Romans tells us:

> *Do not be conformed to this world, but be transformed by the renewing of your mind, that you may prove what is that good and acceptable and perfect will of God* (Romans 12:2).

Some call this process sanctification or consecration. The Lord has always sought to have intimate friendship with His creation, humankind (see Gen. 3:8). What we are really talking about is being transformed into a royal priest according to the order of Melchizedek. To put it in layman's terms, we are all called to be good friends with God.

As we allow the Lord to renew our minds and mindsets, we will see the heavens open over our lives. This, in turn, will give us free access to the domain where angels minister, dance, and worship. We will receive God's perfect plans for our lives and ministry assignments. Our minds will become renewed, realigned (or set upon things above) to another world and an ever-present but hidden spiritual realm where angels are actively working on God's behalf to bring the Lord's purposes to pass on the earth. We see a prophetic picture of this in the life of Joshua.

OUR SUPERNATURAL INHERITANCE

The apostle Peter understood his inheritance of the supernatural and the realms of angels. Remember, we have seen how Peter was broken out of prison by an angel. Look at what Peter encourages us to be as joint heirs of Christ:

> *Blessed be the God and Father of our Lord Jesus Christ, who according to His abundant mercy has begotten us again to a living hope through the resurrection of Jesus Christ from the dead, to an inheritance incorruptible and undefiled and that does not fade away, reserved in heaven for you, who are kept by the power of God through faith for salvation ready to be revealed in the last time. In this you greatly rejoice, though now for a little while, if need be, you have been grieved by various trials, that the genuineness of your faith, being much more precious than gold that perishes, though it is tested by fire, may be found to praise, honor, and glory at the revelation of Jesus Christ, whom having not seen you love. Though now you do not see Him, yet believing, you rejoice with joy inexpressible and full of glory (1 Peter 1:3-8).*

Peter encourages us that our true inheritance is laid up for each of us in Heaven. He also tells us that our faith is more precious than gold and will be tested by fire. That is the season that many find themselves in today. Many people find their faith in God tried as by fire. Can we continue to walk in a form of godliness, denying the power of God? The answer is no. God is calling His people to be refined by holy fire and to walk in holiness and to be transformed into royal priests after the order of Melchizedek. We must submit to the fiery forge of the Holy Spirit as He is bringing His cleansing fire and healing into our lives and hearts. Only when we have submitted to His purging and cleansing will we emerge triumphant and truly prepared to move to the next level of power and anointing the Lord has laid up for those who press through to become true friends of the Father. These fellow servants of Christ Jesus will function as royal priests according to the order of Melchizedek.

I would suggest that you consider praying King David's prayer found in Psalm 51. David was calling out for the Lord to restore their friendship after he had sinned and was separated from God. Many are in this position today. David was desperate to have God's friendship and the precious Holy Spirit in his life. Here is his prayer:

> *Create in me a clean heart, O God, and renew a steadfast spirit within me. Do not cast me away from Your presence, and do not take Your Holy Spirit from me. Restore to me the joy of Your salvation, and uphold me by Your generous Spirit. Then I will teach transgressors Your ways, and sinners shall be converted to You. Deliver me from the guilt of bloodshed, O God, the God of my salvation, and my tongue shall sing aloud of Your righteousness* (Psalm 51:10-14).

Holiness is not optional. Holiness is critical to become a friend of God. There is no other way. Jesus gave us advice in Revelation 3.

Actually the language that Jesus uses here can be compared to a lawyer who is giving advice to one who is on trial for his life.

> *I counsel you to buy from Me gold refined in the fire, that you may be rich; and white garments, that you may be clothed, that the shame of your nakedness may not be revealed; and anoint your eyes with eye salve, that you may see* (Revelation 3:18).

This is also a shadow of Joshua's supernatural experience in the courtroom of Heaven (see Zech 3:1-10). Joshua's angelic encounter in the heavenly realms is a great parabolic portrait of the role of God's priests who are patterned after Christ's model. The Lord is at this hour raising up a people who will minister unto the Lord as priests and prophets after the order of Melchizedek. They will mediate between a holy God and their fellow man.

Again, the Lord is speaking about holiness when He advises us to purchase gold refined by fire and white garments from Him. The gold speaks of our purified and refined faith, and the white garments speak of our holiness. The Lord Jesus also counsels us to anoint our eyes with eye salve. The anointing of our eyes ensures that we will be given the ability or gifting to see clearly. This is the "seer anointing," and the Lord is releasing this anointing to receive supernatural revelations to His friends at this hour. The Lord is plainly speaking of seeing into the realms of the heavens and the Kingdom of Heaven. Remember that we must be born of both water and of spirit! We need pure faith, true holiness, and eyes anointed to see into the supernatural realm where our true inheritance is waiting for each of us.

LISTENING CAREFULLY TO GOD

As a royal priest according to the order of Melchizedek, you will be able to both hear and see the things of God and His Kingdom very clearly. Remember that these are the benefits of living under an open heaven. An important part of this process is developing your ability to hear the voice of God clearly. It is imperative that God's people learn to hear His voice plainly today, as our very lives could well depend upon it. Again, what we are really talking about is becoming a friend of God. As a friend of God, we will have eyes to see, and we will also have our ears tuned to hear even the slightest whispers of the Holy Spirit. These are both very important to stepping into the calling of the royal priesthood.

The result of becoming a friend of God and seeking to walk in holiness is that we will be enabled to hear God quickly and clearly. Again, this is the fruit of living under an open heaven. This will help us to comply with the greatest commandment according to Christ Jesus. Of course, this also leads to our obedience as we respond to His voice and the Lord's directives quickly.

Remember what Jesus said when He was asked which was the greatest commandment? The Lord responded that we must "Hear God." Then he quoted Deuteronomy 6:4. We see that Jesus answered, saying:

> The first of all the commandments is: "Hear, O Israel, the LORD our God, the LORD is one. And you shall love the LORD your God with all your heart, with all your soul, with all your mind, and with all your strength." This is the first commandment" (Mark 12:29-30).

I feel confident saying that Jesus Christ was telling the people that holiness was very important, but that hearing God speak is paramount in our relationship with our heavenly Father.

Learning to walk in holiness and obedience is a process. Recently, I saw a vision of a beautiful little child trying to take his first steps and stumbling. I saw the proud father tenderly pick the child up and place him upright on his clumsy little feet. This happened time and time again. With this vision came understanding. Our heavenly Father smiles and takes great delight in us as we seek to crawl and then take our first steps along the highway of holiness. I feel certain that, at times, we all seek to walk in holiness and total obedience, but we all fall short of the glory of God (see Rom. 3:23). In His wisdom and patience, the Lord was teaching me that we must learn to walk in holiness and obedience in much the same manner that a toddler learns to crawl and then to walk. We are now in a season of grace to learn and be taught by our Father and the precious Holy Spirit. They are Teachers of great patience and kindness. The Lord is preparing His children and friends for a great battle by helping us to learn to walk in true holiness and quick obedience to His calls and beckoning (see John 14:26). The Lord will soon require His friends to run and battle with agility and dexterity.

We have entered into a God-ordained moment of time in which the Lord is opening the heavens over His people and allowing them to access the heavenly realms. This is also the result of the restoration of the gift of discerning of spirits. As we begin to embrace this dynamic of the Kingdom of God, we can begin to experience a greatly increased amount of supernatural activity in our lives. This will include angelic visitations and encounters. In the next chapter, I will share a dramatic supernatural experience and angelic encounter that illustrates one aspect of the priesthood of all believers. Hopefully this testimony will encourage you and help you to understand how this dynamic of living under open heavens may look in your life. It will also give you an idea of what it might look like to function as a royal priest according to the order of Melchizedek. Remember that Christ passed through the heavens in His role as a royal priest after the order of Melchizedek, and we can too. Jesus has blazed a trail into the heavens for you and me. As a result, we can also blaze trails into the heavens and come boldly before God's very throne of mercy and grace. The next testimony may help you understand what it might look like to pass though the open heavens and actually come boldly to the throne of grace.

Chapter 14

ANOINTED TO REIGN AS PRIESTS AND PROPHETS

I n April 2007, I lived through a series of supernatural experiences in Kansas City, Missouri.[1] During this period, I was ministering at Christ Triumphant Church in Lee's Summit, Missouri, where King of Glory Ministries International had sponsored a school of the supernatural. I had shared the message that I was given during that season about approaching global revivals and the importance of angelic ministry's role in sparking these approaching events. I encouraged the people to examine their hearts in preparation for these unfolding events. In the last session, I spoke about how the Lord would begin to allow and anoint ordinary people to ascend into the realms of Heaven and interact with angels to release God's plans upon the earth. During this lesson in the school, I was teaching about third heaven intercession and interacting with open heavens to release or activate angelic intervention and ministry upon the earth.

Some people call these kinds of experiences or angelic encounters and the resulting impact upon the earth "third heaven intercession." When you encounter angels in the heavenly realms, the Lord will often loose these angels to impact your life or your sphere of influence or sphere of anointing. In Zechariah 3, we read a description of such a supernatural experience where Joshua stands in the councils of God. He is standing in the realms of Heaven among Jesus, the Father, and several angels. The Angel of the Lord (Jesus) commands the angels nearby to minister to Joshua. The angels who are in attendance then minister to Joshua by placing upon him a new mantle. This is parabolic of the removal of his sin. The angel places upon him a new mantle that releases forgiveness and cleansing. The new mantle also releases an anointing to complete his calling and mandates from the Lord. This is an area or facet of angelic ministry that the Lord will begin to open up to many people at this hour. I want to elucidate on this passage in this chapter.

We find the impact of Joshua's open heaven experience outlined in the books of Haggai and Zechariah. Joshua was one of the men—along with the prophet Zerubbabel—called to undertake the momentous task of rebuilding the temple in or around 539 B.C. At this hour, God is calling regular people to undertake a similar task of reestablishing His Kingdom upon the earth today. A study of Haggai and Zechariah also reveals the ongoing angelic intervention and involvement in the rebuilding of the Jewish Temple. I suggest it here for your study. However, I believe that the open heaven experience and angelic encounter that we see in Zechariah 3 played a crucial role in the release of the Jews from Babylonian bondage and the restoration of the Temple in Jerusalem. This is a great parabolic portrait of how the Lord will begin to utilize angelic ministry to rebuild or reestablish His Kingdom upon the earth at this hour. Just like Joshua, people today will benefit from and employ angelic ministry. The Lord is beginning to release to His friends the wisdom and understanding of how we can co-labor with His angelic hosts to complete the seemingly impossible task of establishing Christ's Kingdom upon the earth through the work of our hands and the decrees of our lips. The Lord will continue to use individuals in this manner today as well, by allowing ordinary people to co-labor with angels to impact the events and affairs of men upon the earth in every nation and among every tribe and tongue.

We see this type of God-ordained prayer or third heaven intercession and ability to co-labor with God's angels in this passage of Scripture:

> *Then the Angel of the LORD admonished Joshua, saying, "Thus says the LORD of hosts: 'If you will walk in My ways, and if you will keep My command, then you shall also judge My house, and likewise have charge of My courts; I will give you places to walk among these who stand here* [the angels]. *Hear, O Joshua, the high priest, you and your companions who sit before you, for they are a wondrous sign; for behold, I am bringing forth My Servant the BRANCH'"* (Zechariah 3:6-8).

We should remember that Joshua's companions are of the Levitical priesthood, and the angels present in the heavenly realm. On the other hand, we are called to be priests after the order of Melchizedek.

The phrase used in this passage, *"have charge of My courts,"* can literally be translated as "to have free access to the courts or realms of Heaven." The Greek word used here for "have charge" is actually the word *shamar*, and it can be translated as:

> Guard, generally to protect, to attend or to have access to; to be aware of, be circumspect or knowledgeable about a thing, take heed of one's authority for; to keep as a caretaker; to mark or recognize a thing; to look narrowly, to observe, to preserve, to regard, to reserve; to save (self); to wait upon (like a waiter in a fine restaurant), or to watch for or to be a watchmen.[2]

To expound upon this another way, it may be said that you have been freely given the grace to be a witness in God's heavenly courtroom.

This kind of third heaven angelic ministry will markedly increase in the coming seasons. This will be in part because of the Lord's wooing of the Body of Christ, and also because many saints will discern and heed the Lord's urgent call to cleanse their hearts and lives, seeking to walk in true holiness. They will begin a radical search for Jesus with all of their hearts, souls, and minds. As they submit to the Holy Spirit's cleansing and holy fire, they will begin to experience open heavens over their lives and will begin to have free access or charge of the courts of Heaven or heavenly places. In these places, angelic encounters will be plentiful and actually a commonplace event.

These kinds of angelic encounters can be life-changing. Usually these kinds of open heaven angelic encounters will also have a definite and dramatic effect upon the unfolding events on the earth. At times the impact can be immediate, or it can unfold chronologically. Nonetheless, these kind of third heaven angelic encounters are very important and will affect the earth in the coming days.

This will surely be true concerning the approaching global revivals and outpourings of God's Spirit and power. Again, the ability and privilege to enter into the heavenly realms and co-labor with Christ's angels will be characteristic of the priesthood of all believers in the coming days.

THE COURTS OF HEAVEN

When the school of the supernatural was completed, I returned to the church the next day to finalize some chores. It was a Monday, and the building was empty. As I unlocked the front door and walked past the double doors to the sanctuary, I sensed the power of the Holy Spirit hovering around the altar. I had stood on that altar and preached this message from Zechariah 3 and God's invitation to His people to access the heavenly courtroom just about 12 hours before. In my mind, I knew that I needed to do those chores that would take about an hour. I was preparing to depart on an international ministry trip to Sweden, Holland, and the United Kingdom the next morning, so I was on a tight schedule. I was in a hurry. I was busy. But my spirit was drawn to the presence of the Lord that was hanging heavily in the sanctuary. I said, "Lord, what do You want me to do?"

I heard the Lord say, "Come up here." I thought that the Holy Spirit was referring to the altar in the church sanctuary. So I walked slowly through the edifice and knelt at a spot at the middle of the altar.

It seemed that the heavens were open overhead, and I could feel the Holy Spirit swirling in and around the altar and platform. Then I heard beautiful worship music, and for a moment thought that perhaps Pastor Joe Gabbard might be in the sound booth. I turned to check and saw only flashes of light shooting through the building. I said, "Lord, what are You doing this morning, and what do You want me to do?"

Once more I heard the Lord say, "Come up here." I had the revelation that I needed to lay prostrate upon a certain spot of the gray carpet. The instant that I was obedient to lay down, I was immediately launched out of my body. This was the same kind of sensation that I had experienced in Newfoundland when I had been taken by a strong angel into the presence of Jesus. It seemed that the Lord was serious when He said, "Come up here." This was another example of the Holy Spirit opening the heavens and working in symphony with angelic ministry.[3]

Again, I sensed that an angel had taken my left hand and was escorting me into the realms of Heaven. When I landed, I came into an immense room full of glory and light. Four angels escorted me to a large, high podium or bench of some type. When I looked up to see the bench, I was blinded by the radiance of the brilliant white light and power that emanated from that spot. I suddenly realized that I was in the place of Zechariah 3. I was standing in the heavenly council room of God. A holy fear gripped me, and I slumped, seeking to fall upon my face, but several angels held me up by my arms and kept me in a standing position. My strength totally evaporated. In the presence of the Lord, I dared not look at the bench nor the brilliant glory and blinding white light that exploded from behind it. I was sure that it was the Father, and I was also certain that if I looked at Him I would die.

Suddenly I was aware that an extraordinary multitude of angelic beings were surrounding this room and that there was worship and singing that venerated the Lamb of God. However, I was too terrified to enjoy the thousands of angels that were present or to concentrate upon the ethereal music. In this place, I was instantly aware of my sinful nature and the self-seeking agendas hidden deep within my heart. A holy fear of eternal damnation permeated my spirit, and I was terrified of what might happen next. In the next instant, I heard a railing voice making all sorts of accusations about me.

As I raised my head a little to see who was speaking, I caught a glimpse of a mighty right hand moving violently down from the midst of the glory of the throne (or what may have been the judgment seat of God). I was gripped with the pure fear of the Lord. Suddenly the Father's right hand slammed down a wooden gavel with ornate golden inlaid trim. Immediately there was an ear-splitting crack of thunder, and lightning shot from the place that the gavel had made contact with the podium. Instantly, it was silent save for the sound of harps gently playing in the glory around the judgment seat.

Then I saw Jesus. He stepped forward and began to speak to the Father, though I was unable to understand the language that He spoke. The Lord spoke for several minutes. During this time the holy fear had lifted from my spirit a little, and I dared to look around at my surroundings a teeny bit. Somehow I knew that Jesus was, at that moment, arguing my case before the Father the way a lawyer might present a client's defense in a court on earth. I turned to the left to see my Lord. For the first time since I had arrived in this place, I was able to feel Christ's total and unparalleled love for me. I felt the power of His unconditional love the same way that I had first experienced it when Jesus had called me to Him in prayer the first time. That was the time that He told me that he was appointing four angels to me. Now these same four angels encircled me and were holding me in a standing position with their powerful hands. I was experiencing the sensation of Christ's love the same way that I did the time the Lord stood over me in Living Waters Church in Springdale, Newfoundland, Canada. The love and grace of God that exuded from Jesus at that moment gave me hope that I might live and not die. I began to get a little courage to examine the environment in more detail.

As Jesus spoke to the Father on my behalf, I looked at the judgment seat or podium again. The glory of the Father was still radiating from that place in brilliance, and there were sweeping and swirling circles of phosphorescent colors radiating from His presence. There were also several large creatures that resembled human-sized hummingbirds that appeared to have multiple wings. These creatures appeared to be flying together in a loose formation around the podium and through the phosphorescent glory. These creatures appeared to be worshipping as they zipped through and fluttered supernaturally quickly around the throne, and they seemed to be dispersing this tangible, phosphorescent glory of the Most High God as they whizzed past. It is possible that they may have been seraphim. The brilliance of these waves of color caused my eyes to ache. Still, I was too fearful to look for longer than a fleeting second. The podium was massive and seemed to be at least 25 or 30 feet high and very long. It was difficult to determine the size because of the brilliance of the glory that was emanating from the Father as it obscured the podium. It appeared to be fashioned of fine, polished wood and was inlaid with intricate works and designs of gold.

As I turned my head to the left and right, I could see what appeared to be literally millions of angelic beings who were watching these events unfold. This plethora of angels were all garbed in immaculate white robes and sat in a massive circle around the throne of God. I was mesmerized. Standing in a semi-circle around me were four familiar angels. About two dozen angelic beings were seated nearby. They were all robed in shining white garments. When I made eye contact with one of my friends, one of the angels beside me, he smiled at me with reassurance. However, I was still in a state of fear and shock that I was actually in this place that I had preached and prophesied about just a few hours earlier. I was aware of the immaculate white marble floor that I was standing on. It felt very clean and cool to my bare feet.

When Jesus finished His oration, there was another incredibly loud clap of thunder as the Father slammed the podium once more with His gavel. Lightening bolted through the massive room and it was silent again, save for the harps. Suddenly, the Father spoke. This both surprised me and brought another round of fear into my heart. He said, "What say you?" Then I began to hear the enemy. I looked to my right and saw satan. He was bringing railing accusations against me. He was quite angry, and he was very animated. He was jumping up and down and screaming, "Those souls are mine. He cannot have them!"

The evil one turned and pointed a bony finger in my direction and continued to scream and bring more and more accusations and lies against me. At that moment I was in complete surprise at his appearance. In this place he looked quite harmless, and I had the revelation that it is through subterfuge, deception, fear, and lies that he convinces humans that he is powerful and fierce. In fact, he is not. In this place it is apparent that he is defeated. For a moment, I considered laughing at his accusations and lies, but I was also aware of the fact that would have been improper here. However, I did allow a small smile to rise up in my spirit. When this happened, the angel that was standing on my left holding my arm looked at me sternly. I lowered my head and began to wonder just exactly what I was experiencing.

From time to time, I would glimpse at the glory surrounding the Father's judgment seat, but I was too fearful to look for longer than a short second. As I peeked up, I saw the Father's mighty right hand slam the gavel down onto the podium again. Once more, lightning bolts flew from the spot through the massive room, and thunder roared in my ears. When the thundering subsided, it was silent again, save for the ethereal sound of the harps. As the echoes of the thunderings subsided, the Father spoke: "Enough." His voice shook the colossal building, and I could not help but notice the evil one cower and tremble in fear. I looked up at the glory that was emanating from the podium and the place where the hand of the Father had emerged from it. For a split nanosecond, I was able to behold His glory, and I was filled with awe and delight at the utter splendor and majesty of the Lord. I did not actually see the Father, only His glory.

At that moment, the Father broke the silence, saying, "What say you?" I noticed that Jesus had turned and was looking at me, as were the angels that were in attendance. Then I realized that God was asking me to speak!

For an instant, my eyes locked with the beautiful eternal eyes of the Messiah, and I had instant revelation and said, "I ask not for the one million souls; but now I ask You, Father, for two million souls." When I said this, the evil one began to have a tantrum and started foaming at the mouth and screaming at the podium once more. The evil one was jumping around like a flea on a hot ash pile.

Once more I saw the Father's mighty right hand appear through the glory cloud of His throne of judgment and grace to slam the gavel down all over again. As His hand appeared, He bellowed, "Silence!" Once more thunder and lightning bolts flew throughout the massive room, and after a moment, it was silent again. Only the ethereal sound of the harps was present. I saw the evil one trembling and crouched in fear. Then the Father said, "Granted! Let it be so!" At that moment I saw a strong angel begin to write in a massive book. This powerful angel was seated at one end of the Father's throne of grace or judgment seat.

When this happened, one of the attendant angels stepped up behind me and removed my robe. He took it and handed it to a second angel. For a moment I saw the robe that I had been wearing. For the first time I noticed that it was filthy, spotted, and ugly. Then a third attendant angel stepped forward and handed the first angel a fresh, clean, glimmering white robe. The first angel then placed the new robe upon my shoulders, and I smiled as I felt the power of the Holy Spirit course through my being. Suddenly I felt wholeness and cleansing that I had never experienced before. I turned to thank the angel and saw Jesus smiling brightly with approval of my new robe.

Then the Father said, "Say on," and I was aware that I was able to continue to make requests in the very presence of God. At this point, I am not going to share anything further from this parabolic heavenly vision except to say that I was allowed to ask the Father for several things as the vision unfolded. These are special pearls and personal treasures that I keep and ponder in my heart. However, I will say that some things I requested were granted and sealed in Heaven as I saw the Father's mighty right hand descend each time to His throne of judgment and slam His gavel down saying, "Granted. Let it be so." And each time I saw a strong angel begin to write in a massive book. There were two things that I requested that were not granted. These were also sealed with a mighty stroke of the gavel and accompanying thunders and lightning and recorded by the scribe angel in the massive books. I am not certain why two of my requests were not granted. I had asked these for other people. Perhaps I had asked amiss (see James 4:3). Or perhaps those folks are required to make their requests personally. It is also possible that the timing of my requests were off. Honestly, I do not know the exact reason why.

When my session came to a conclusion, I was aware that it was time for me to depart from this place, as there was other pressing business at hand or on the docket that day. I turned to see Jesus smile at me one last time. I had a strong desire to take a few steps to my left and reach out to touch Him as I had done in the past. However, I realized that was not appropriate here. Jesus was wearing a white tallit, or prayer shawl, over His shoulders and the tassels were a material composed of shimmering gold. They gently swayed just below His waist. I suddenly had the revelation that the Christ is a royal priest forever after the order of Melchizedek. Christ had accomplished His mission of opening the heavens over humankind. Because of this, we can enter freely into the heavenly realms and actually come boldly before the throne of grace.

The strong angel that was standing by my left side took my left hand, and suddenly I was traveling back through time and space again. I could feel my spirit accelerating and saw the earth come into view below. What a majestic planet! The clouds swirled and the seas appeared to be brilliant emerald green in places. (I thought to myself, "I would really like to go snorkeling there.") In a few seconds, we passed through the outer atmosphere of the earth, and I saw North America. Then I recognized the Mississippi River. Almost immediately I was free falling directly at the roof of Christ Triumphant Church. I turned to my left to see the strong angel smile at me one last time, and I reentered my body, which I could see lying at the foot of the altar.

I began to weep, and I noticed that my body was covered with sweat. The presence of Jesus still clung to me, and I lay upon the spot for a long time and wept greatly as I pondered these things in my heart. I could smell frankincense, and could still feel Christ's love radiating over me. As I lay there on the carpet, I could still hear harps and ethereal angelic voices singing in some unknown tongue, but that no longer surprised me.

After this open heaven encounter, I seemed to be in a state of rapture for several days. I seemed to sleepwalk through the preparations for the trip to Europe. On the flight to Europe, I was in constant prayer, seeking the Lord for an explanation for these supernatural events. I remembered the prophetic decrees that I had spoken the final night of the school of the supernatural, and I had the understanding that the Lord had allowed me to personally experience the message I had shared. This kind of interaction with open heavens is a reality for people today. Again, you need not be a chosen vessel or a member of the fivefold ministry. The Lord is calling his friends to "Come up here" in a similar way that he did with John the Revelator. We have the authority to appropriate the spiritual principle found in Revelation 4 at this crucial hour:

> *After these things I looked, and behold, a door standing open in heaven. And the first voice which I heard was like a trumpet speaking with me, saying, "Come up here, and I will show you things which must take place after this"* (Revelation 4:1).

The Lord is inviting His friends to ascend through the *"door standing open in heaven"* or through open heavens. That is the hour that we are in. There is free access into the courts of God and other heavenly places. When we understand this and prepare ourselves to attend the courts of Heaven, we will be shown the things that God has ordained to *"take place after this."* For me, I believe that the Lord has promised that I will be given the grace to be responsible for seeing 2,000,000 salvations through the work of my hands as I walk in obedience to His Spirit. This will happen in some fashion. How this will unfold, I am not sure. However, I have the promise, and I trust the Father to bring it to pass. The only thing that I need to do is to listen carefully and learn to *hear*. I need to learn to watch carefully and learn to *see*. Then I need to be obedient to God's Spirit and do those things that I see and hear. Perhaps these would be good things for you to practice also. Perhaps the Lord is calling you to do some things too. Perhaps the Lord is calling you to *"Come up here"* too. Perhaps you *can* access the realms of Heaven and co-labor with God's angels therein. What would you ask God for?

To accomplish this, we will need to fulfill the requirements that are laid out in Revelation 3. Before the invitation to "Come up here" was given to John, there were prerequisites established when Jesus said:

> *Behold, I stand at the door and knock. If anyone hears My voice and opens the door, I will come in to him and dine with him, and he with Me. To him who overcomes I will grant to sit with Me on My throne, as I also overcame and sat down with My Father on His throne. "He who has an ear, let him hear what the Spirit says to the churches"* (Revelation 3:20-22).

Jesus is telling us that we have a part to play in opening the heavens. We can be transformed into overcomers. We can minister as priests after the order of Melchizedek. First it is necessary to hear His voice, because the Lord is telling us at times He still stands at the door and knocks today. What door? The door of your heart. Yes, perhaps, but more importantly, it is the door that opens the heavens over our lives. We have been given the keys to open the door or heavens over our lives through the finished work of Christ on Calvary's Tree. This supernatural key comes when we hear His voice and seek to cleanse ourselves in preparation to ascend into the courts and realms of Heaven.

We can now access the realms of Heaven to gain revelation and implement or release the Kingdom of Heaven on earth in our spheres of influence. This is possible because Jesus Christ came and opened the heavens over humankind. The Lord modeled for us how the priesthood after the order of Melchizedek would function and minister. We can emulate Jesus and pass through the heavens according to the principle of Hebrews 4:

> *Seeing then that we have a great High Priest who has passed through the heavens, Jesus the Son of God, let us hold fast our confession* (Hebrews 4:14).

It is possible for you and me to come boldly to the throne of grace that we may obtain mercy and find grace to help us in our time of need. This will empower us to minister Christ's love and establish His Kingdom in our spheres of influence. We can access the realms of Heaven just as Christ modeled for you and me. The author of Hebrews had supernatural revelation about this aspect of the new covenant that Christ forged for you and me upon the Cross of Calvary. Jesus purchased this aspect of our inheritance with His own precious blood. In the next chapter, we will look at this role in more detail.

ENDNOTES

1. I have shared these in great detail in *Dancing With Angels 1*, Chapters 18-20.

2. Strong, James. *Strong's Exhaustive Concordance of the Bible.* Peabody, MA: Hendrickson Publishers, 2007. #8104.

3. See *Dancing With Angels 1,* Chapter 3.

Chapter 15

UNDERSTANDING YOUR ROLE AS A ROYAL PRIEST AFTER THE ORDER OF MELCHIZEDEK

Earlier we looked at some of the Scripture teachings about Melchizedek. In his teachings in the book of Hebrews, the author quotes Psalm 110. I personally believe that it was the apostle Paul who penned Hebrews, because in my opinion he had a divine revelation of the Messiah's role as the Royal Priest after the order of Melchizedek. This is a matter that is open to debate, but I hold to this opinion.

I want to look at these Scriptures in more detail to help us to understand our role as royal priests after the order of Melchizedek. Psalm 110 gives us a more detailed description and more information about the dynamics or characteristics of the duties of the royal priesthood after the order of Melchizedek. Let's examine this passage: *"The LORD said to my Lord, 'Sit at My right hand, till I make Your enemies Your footstool'"* (Ps. 110:1).

We need to understand the magnitude of the invitation given to us here. Yes, this was spoken to Christ by the Father. However, in the prophetic anointing King David was writing in, he also spoke these words and promises to you and me as joint heirs with Christ. The Scripture is alive. We are born to grow and to mature into the very image of Christ. We are designed to have our minds renewed and transformed into Christ-like minds. King David, who was a type of royal priest after the order of Melchizedek, penned these words for you and me, too. Remember that David was both a king and a priest, which are two of the most important attributes of the royal priests after the order of Melchizedek. He carried power, anointing, and authority in the spiritual realm and also in the natural realm. King David understood this dynamic.

ROYAL AUTHORITY

When God invites you to sit down at His right hand, He is asking you to sit down in unity and friendship with Him at His seat of power, both in the spirit and the natural realm. To sit at the right hand of God means to sit with Him and His hand of power, flexibility, or dexterity.[1] He is calling us to sit beside Him upon His throne of power and glory. Jesus taught us in Matthew 5:34 that God's throne is in Heaven. And we see in Hebrews that we are to fashion our faith after Christ's example:

> *Looking unto Jesus, the author and finisher of our faith, who for the joy that was set before Him endured the cross, despising the shame, and has sat down at the right hand of the throne of God* (Hebrews 12:2).

And again, this Scripture confirms that through Christ's finished work upon Calvary He was and is seated by the Father's right hand of power and authority. We have been given this same freedom and access to God's throne of grace and power through the atonement. We *can* sit with God in heavenly places today (see Eph. 1:3; 2:6).

In the second half of Psalm 110:1, we are told the fruit of being seated at the very right hand of God: *"Till I make Your enemies Your footstool."* This is a beautiful portrait of the royal priesthood after the order of Melchizedek. God will conquer and vanquish our enemies on our behalf! Not only that, but the Father will also place our enemies under our feet. The truth is that our total triumph and victory over our foes is already finished. The enemy of our soul is already defeated and is, in fact, under our feet. We just need to get the revelation of this fact, and then we need to begin to walk it out in the temporal or earthly realm. An important key to this is just realizing that we have the liberty to access the heavenly places and obtain God's revelation, power, and delegated authority.

Look at Psalm 110:2: *"The LORD shall send the rod of Your strength out of Zion. Rule in the midst of Your enemies!"* I find this Scripture fascinating. The Father will send out the rod of Christ's strength from Zion, and the result will be ruling over our enemies. In this passage, the word "rod" also means "scepter." The scepter represents the delegated authority of the King. This is the instrument that symbolizes a royal king's authority and rule. The rod obviously represents Christ; however, it also symbolizes the power and authority of Zion or the Church that God is raising up to rule and reign. The word "rod" can also be translated as a tribe or the tribe.[2]

In essence, the rod or scepter that will be in the Father's hand will be a tribe that He will raise up from within Zion or the Body of Christ. The Lord raised up the Levitical priesthood from the tribe of Levi under the old covenant. At this hour, He is busy raising up a new order of priests from the tribe of the Lion of Judah. The Lord is raising up a royal priesthood after the order of Melchizedek who will rule and reign with the power and authority of the Father's scepter in their hands. This is a great privilege, and the Lord will not allow just anyone to minister or operate in this kind of anointing or heavenly power. You could call this the mantle of the royal priesthood after the order of Melchizedek. It is a precious thing that the Father sent His only Son to establish upon the earth. In essence, we are speaking about a God-ordained or *kairos* moment of time when the Lord will freely give His power to His friends.

We see this in the next verse:

Your people shall be volunteers in the day of Your power;
in the beauties of holiness, from the womb of the morning,
You have the dew of Your youth (Psalm 110:3).

The language here actually speaks of a set time when an army of God will be cloaked in holiness. The terms "from the womb" and "dew of youth" do not necessarily refer to a chronological age or natural birth. They refer to a rebirth of the spirit, or as Jesus actually said, a set time when Christ's people will be born from above or born from the realms of Heaven. It is speaking of a rebirth of the mind and the spirit. This passage refers to an army or chosen tribe of God's champions who will be given free access to ascend through the open heavens, which Christ has restored to humankind, to sit at the right hand of God in holiness, kingly authority, and supernatural power. Verse 4 summarizes this promise and the definition of this free gift from our Father: *"The*

LORD has sworn and will not relent, 'You are a priest forever according to the order of Melchizedek'" (Ps. 110:4).

You are called to be a royal priest after the order of Melchizedek who will rule and reign with the power and authority of the Father's throne. These dynamics are manifesting upon the earth today and have begun to accelerate at this hour. Christ has given us an example to emulate. We are to extend the dominion of Christ's Kingdom as a royal priesthood after the order of Melchizedek who will rule and reign with the power and authority of Heaven upon the earth. Zechariah also paints a portrait of this role of Christ:

> Thus says the LORD of hosts, saying: "Behold, the Man whose name is the BRANCH! From His place He shall branch out, and He shall build the temple of the LORD; yes, He shall build the temple of the LORD. He shall bear the glory, and shall sit and rule on His throne; so He shall be a priest on His throne, and the counsel of peace shall be between them both" (Zechariah 6:12-13).

This refers to Christ and His Bride ministering as a mediator between the heavenly realm and the temporal or earthly realm. Again, this is yet another facet of the royal priesthood after the order of Melchizedek to rule and reign with the delegated power of God's throne of power and grace.

We are also called to be priests upon the throne, and Psalm 110 illustrates this dynamic:

> The Lord is at Your right hand; He shall execute kings in the day of His wrath. He shall judge among the nations, He shall fill the places with dead bodies, He shall execute the heads of many countries. He shall drink

of the brook by the wayside; therefore He shall lift up the head (Psalm 110:5-7).

Again, God will conquer our foes and fight our battles if we allow Him.

We can begin to understand our high calling as a priest after the order of Melchizedek. We can begin to enter into the heavenly realms. Then we will begin to see God Almighty fight on our behalf. Very few individuals have ever tapped into this kind of heavenly power and authority. Those who have were all extremely close friends of God. Folks like Moses, Elijah, Enoch, and of course, Christ are all examples of people who operated in the anointing of the mantle of Melchizedek. These folks were not always subject to the laws of nature, and miracles, signs, and wonders were normal for them. Of course, they were just human beings like you and I, too.

In the coming days, there will be times that regular people will be given a similar power over the laws of nature. This supernatural authority will be given from God to His friends for segments of time to help people fulfill a mandate or calling of the Lord. God is preparing a tribe of friends who will not always be not subject to the laws of nature. And at certain God-ordained moments of time, miracles, signs, and wonders will be normal for them, too. These people will not walk in this kind of God-given authority constantly, but at times this mantle of Melchizedek will come upon them to release signs and wonders in the name of Jesus. They will walk in the anointing of a priest and prophet according to the order or mantle of Melchizedek. Supernatural authority, signs, wonders, and miracles will be common for these friends of the living God. You are called to walk in this kind of God-ordained intimacy and power, too, every day, everywhere you go.

That is exactly what God wants for you and me today. The Lord is calling us to "Come up here" into the heavenly realms and to see and hear what must take place after this (see Rev. 4:1). That is the hour that we are living in today. We can have free access to the very throne of God. In the last chapter, I shared one profound example of accessing the heavenly realms to impact the earthly realm. Not all third heaven encounters will be that dramatic. Others will be quite pleasant, refreshing, and edifying. In the next book of this trilogy, *Dancing With Angels 3: Angels in the Realms of Heaven*, I will share many testimonies of these kinds of open heaven or third heaven visitations and describe how Heaven appears. I will also describe the duties of angels and what they are doing in Heaven today. This will help the reader to understand more dynamics of how they can tap into or access the of mantle of Melchizedek

INHERITANCE

In Hebrews 6, we see more details about the mantle or anointing of Melchizedek:

Thus God, determining to show more abundantly to the heirs of promise the immutability of His counsel, confirmed it by an oath, that by two immutable things, in which it is impossible for God to lie, we might have strong consolation, who have fled for refuge to lay hold of the hope set before us. This hope we have as an anchor of the soul, both sure and steadfast, and which enters the Presence behind the veil, where the forerunner has entered for us, even Jesus, having become High Priest forever according to the order of Melchizedek (Hebrews 6:17-20).

In this passage, Paul outlines some of his revelation about the mantle or anointing of Melchizedek. First, Paul encourages us that it is impossible for God to lie. I want to grasp that mentally concerning what I am writing about. God has promised us the ability to enter into the heavenly realms and to tap into the mantle of Melchizedek. This is truth. Paul goes on to inform us that we all have a refuge and an anchor of hope that is real, solid, and unchanging. But what anchor is Paul referring to?

Paul is telling us that we have an immutable and unchangeable promise from our heavenly Father who will never lie to us. What is that promise? That promise is to enter into the very Presence of God by going behind the veil (or through the heavens, the open heavens), coming boldly to the very throne room of God. This is not just flowery language or alliteration. This promise is the truth! The Lord promised you and me the right and ability to enter into the very dwelling place of God, into the holy of holies; that is our anchor. We can go boldly before the very throne of grace and power of God. Why? Because we have an advocate. We have a forerunner. Christ Jesus split open the heavens to restore humankind's relationship with God, and our ability to access heavens and have fellowship, communion, and friendship with Almighty God. Finally, Paul defines this very privilege or attribute in these terms: *"having become High Priest forever according to the order of Melchizedek."*

That is our inheritance. That should be our goal. We need to emulate Christ in this because we are truly called to be a priesthood after the order of Melchizedek who will rule and reign upon the earth. It *is* possible for us to enter into the Presence behind the veil, where the Forerunner has blazed a supernatural trail for us, and to become a high priest forever according to the order of Melchizedek today. We can enter into the heavenly places with

Christ today and obtain a heavenly perspective, heavenly authority, and God-given power to impact our lives and spheres of influence. We can wield the scepter of heavenly power.

Hebrews 12 accurately describes what we should seek to do to emulate Christ's example.

> *Therefore we also, since we are surrounded by so great a cloud of witnesses, let us lay aside every weight, and the sin which so easily ensnares us, and let us run with endurance the race that is set before us, looking unto Jesus, the author and finisher of our faith, who for the joy that was set before Him endured the cross, despising the shame, and has sat down at the right hand of the throne of God* (Hebrews 12:1-2).

We can also embrace our cross and die to our agendas and seek God's perfect will for our lives. We must overcome the sin in our lives that weighs us down to this temporal or carnal realm. In fact, if you hope to experience the mantle or anointing of Melchizedek today, you will need to seek to walk in holiness and sanctification. Holiness is absolutely necessary to become a priest after the order of Melchizedek. You can become a royal priest after the order of Melchizedek, but holiness is not optional. Thankfully, the blood of Christ has made holiness possible for us today. This is because of Christ, who through the eternal Spirit offered Himself without spot to God and has cleansed our conscience from dead works to serve the living God (see Heb. 9:6-14).

To minister in the role or anointing of a royal priesthood after the order of Melchizedek, we must walk in holiness. We must walk blamelessly before our God. The Lord is calling His people to walk in the fullness of Christ's character. In other words, we need to be transformed into the very image of Jesus. Our mind needs to be transformed into a Christ-like mind. Our mindset needs to be transformed into a heavenly mindset. I was once told that I was "so heavenly minded that I was no earthly good." However, I perceived what was meant to be a criticism of me was a great compliment. I don't want to be earthly minded. I want my mind transformed and set upon things above! Really what we are speaking of is a metamorphosis of our spirits and very being as we grow into a mature creature who is shaped and molded into the very image of the Messiah. We can be recreated in God's own image; then we can recreate Christ in our spheres of influence. That is God's ultimate plan for you and me (see Gen. 1:26).

In Romans, the apostle Paul encourages us, saying:

> *I beseech you therefore, brethren, by the mercies of God, that you present your bodies a living sacrifice, holy, acceptable to God, which is your reasonable service. And do not be conformed to this world, but be transformed by the renewing of your mind, that you may prove what is that good and acceptable and perfect will of God* (Romans 12:1-2).

We need to be totally heavenly minded. Paul understood the importance of having our minds renewed or transformed because he also realized that it led to holiness.

Our minds need to be stayed upon Christ and His Kingdom. The transformation of our minds leads to a Christ-like character. It is wise to remember that Saul actually experienced a personal metamorphosis and was transformed into Paul. He forsook riches, position, prestige, power, and even his family to follow Christ. However, the most critical thing that he gave up was his pharisaical mindset. Paul's mind was transformed, and he encourages us that we also need to have our minds transformed. Paul counted everything that he had learned over a lifetime of education and study garbage in order that he might obtain a Christ-like mind. We need that same kind of devotion and mindset today. We need to take up our cross and put away our sinful natures and mental strongholds.

In Second Corinthians, Paul elaborates on this transformation teaching:

> We all, with unveiled face, beholding as in a mirror the glory of the Lord, are being transformed into the same image from glory to glory, just as by the Spirit of the Lord (2 Corinthians 3:18).

He speaks of how the precious Holy Spirit is at work in our hearts and minds, transforming us into the very image of Christ. This is a sovereign and supernatural work of grace. We need to be mindful that the Lord is gently seeking to reshape our hearts, souls, and minds. It would be wise to submit to the refining forge of the Holy Spirit and His purifying process today.

Again, this is the season that many find themselves in at this hour. God is preparing His Bride. The Lord is raising up a royal priesthood after the order of Melchizedek. These friends of God will be holy. They will minister in the mantle or anointing of Melchizedek. They will mediate between earth and Heaven as they realize their supernatural inheritance, understand how to ascend into the heavenly realms, and work in symphony with the Holy Spirit and God's angelic host to impact the events on earth for Christ's Kingdom and His purposes. These friends of God will rend the heavens over their lives and gain free access to the very courtrooms of God. They will have revelation and understand how to work in harmony with the unction of the Holy Spirit to manifest the Kingdom of God. At times, they will be released to co-labor with God's angels.

Jesus is standing at the door of the heavens and knocking. It is our responsibility to hear Him and to answer. He has given you and me authority to release His Kingdom upon the earth as we learn to minister under the open heavens that Christ restored to humankind. We can learn to work in harmony with the Holy Spirit and in symphony with Christ's angelic hosts. The days of the restoration of all things are at hand, and we can now live our lives in the fullness of Christ and His finished work of Calvary and the Lord's total atonement. We can serve a living God in power and authority! It is finished! However, it has just begun!

ENDNOTES

1. Strong, James. *Strong's Exhaustive Concordance of the Bible.* Peabody, MA: Hendrickson Publishers, 2007. #H3225.
2. *Ibid.* #H4292.

God has given every person the ability and opportunity to grow in the grace and knowledge of our Lord and Savior Jesus Christ. What a glorious thing the Lord has done! God has sent His only begotten Son to humanity to restore the communion and fellowship that is our inheritance. The Messiah has reinstated the open heavens over us and given us the opportunity to ascend through those open heavens and to enter into His very presence. Jesus has reestablished humanity's inheritance—communion with God Almighty. We can walk in fellowship with God just as Adam and Eve in the Garden of Eden, because Jesus has opened the heavens over humankind once and for all.

Once we get the revelation that it *is* possible for us to overcome and to *"lay aside every weight, and the sin"* that tethers or binds us to the carnal or temporal realm, we can begin to enter into a wonderful communion and fellowship with God. We can access the open heavens and sit with Christ in heavenly places. Hebrews tells us this:

> *Therefore we also, since we are surrounded by so great a cloud of witnesses, let us lay aside every weight, and the sin which so easily ensnares us, and let us run with*

endurance the race that is set before us, looking unto Jesus, the author and finisher of our faith [through the Atonement], *who for the joy that was set before Him endured the cross, despising the shame, and has sat down at the right hand of the throne of God* (Hebrews 12:1-2).

This passage gives us another wonderful example of Christ's ministry for us to follow or emulate, and it also gives us the key that will empower us to pursue or go after Him. Christ overcame sin for us and empowered you and me to rise into the heavenly places with Him.

WE ARE SEATED WITH CHRIST

The Scriptures give us a wonderful promise in Ephesians: "[God has] *raised us up together, and made us sit together in the heavenly places in Christ Jesus*" (Eph. 2:6). We are seated with Christ. This was already established and finished by Christ's triumphant work of atonement on the Cross. Notice that this Scripture is in the past tense. We are already seated with Christ in heavenly places. It does not say that we are going to be seated with Christ after we complete a sufficient amount of work or become "worthy" enough to enter God's presence. No. Because of Christ's shed blood, you and I are now seated with Christ. It has already happened. It is a done deal!

Our place and spiritual inheritance is one of ruling and reigning with Christ in the heavenly places. We are seated in a position of power, authority, and honor. We are triumphant (see 2 Cor. 2:14)! Because we believe that Christ is the Messiah through simple faith in His atoning work, this is our inheritance now, today. You can have it. When Jesus overcame death and was seated by the right hand of the Father in triumph over the devil, we were also seated in this heavenly place of power and kingly authority. We are royal priests after the order of Melchizedek.

The Weymouth translation tells us that God, *"Raised us with Him from the dead, and enthroned us with Him in the heavenly realms as being in Christ Jesus"* (Eph. 2:6 WNT). The Father has enthroned us in the heavenly places with Christ Jesus! It is finished. We are victorious and triumphant in Christ as we begin to appropriate the revelation that we are seated with Christ or *enthroned* with Christ in the heavenly places. We are seated as joint heirs or joint kings with Christ. We are His ambassadors with His authority, power, and triumph. We are able to rule and reign in this life!

We have the privilege and God-granted right to benefit from, enjoy, and luxuriate in our joint seating with Christ in heavenly places. This is a position and place of victory and the place of God's overcomers! When we sit down with Christ in the heavenly places, we are seated in victory over all powers and principalities of this world. Our minds will be stayed upon the Messiah, and we will be given God's perfect double peace (see Isa. 26:3). Not only that, but we will walk in power over our foes. You can have this position in Christ. It has already happened because Jesus achieved this victory for us to make us joint heirs with Christ in the heavenly realms or places. When we begin to appropriate and walk in this revelation of our position in Christ, it will transform our lives! We will be able to walk in the commanded blessing and anointing of Ephesians 2:7:

> *That in the ages to come He might show the exceeding riches of His grace in His kindness toward us in Christ Jesus.*

We will be authorized to display or manifest Christ's Kingdom. We will be empowered to do the greater works that Jesus has called us to work (see John 14:12). We will evolve and metamorphose into the victorious and triumphant people God has preordained for His children to become.

REVELATION FOR GOD'S OVERCOMERS

The key is the revelation of the Messiah's atonement that enables us to overcome the weight of sin that tethers us to the carnal or temporal realm. This supernatural knowledge or understanding comes to us easily once we have managed to open the heavens over our lives with the help and guidance of the Holy Spirit. Once Christ's finished work becomes real or alive in our spirit man, we can follow Him to the same place that He ascended to, the very presence or throne room of God. In that place, we will find the power to triumph and be transformed into overcomers (see Rev. 3:21-22).

However, many of us are just like Cleopas (see Luke 24:18-33). We are carnal minded and spiritual babes in our revelatory knowledge of Christ's atonement and His Kingdom. Even though we have the revealed Word of God and Christ has actually visited and continues to visit the earth to reveal to us this Good News, many people have no idea that we can walk in harmony with God. Few of us understand the ramifications and outworking of the atonement that the Messiah purchased for us on the Cross. But the Lord wants us to have this revelation, and we are living in the day when He will begin to make this knowledge and understanding of the Messiah's atonement readily available to His creation—you and me. As the heavens open over our lives, we too will come to the place where we will say, "Our heart burns within us as He talks to us and opens the Scriptures for us" (see Luke 24:32). The Lord will begin to reveal and release supernatural revelation to His people as the heavens are opening in this hour, and many will go boldly through the open heavens to join Christ in heavenly places, *enthroned* at the right hand of the Father.

The Lord has restored His good treasure—the open heavens—to His creation, humankind. We are living in the day that the fulfillment of the prophetic promise given to us by God in Deuteronomy has come to pass. *"The LORD will open to you His good treasure, the heavens..."* (Deut. 28:12). The heavens have been opened by God Himself. We can pass through the heavens like Jesus (see Acts 1:9-10; Heb. 4:14). We are called to be royal priests after the order of Melchizedek. We *can* come boldly before God's throne of grace and power. We can enter into the open heavens and obtain supernatural revelation that we can implement upon the earth to manifest Messiah's Kingdom according to Christ's model (see Luke 11:2; Matt. 6:10).

I want to point out that you do not to have to have extraordinary supernatural experiences like those I have shared in this book to work with God's angels. I have chosen the testimonies that I placed in this book because they make for "good reading." They also serve to stir up your spirit as you read them, and hopefully they will encourage you to seek God for similar encounters.

However, as we mature and begin to understand more about the idiosyncrasies of Christ's Kingdom, we will become adept at working with God's angels in our everyday lives. As we learn to work in symphony with the Holy Spirit, our spirits will become fine-tuned to recognize the unction of the Holy Spirit when He is moving in our spheres of influence. The Lord will help us understand how to recognize the nuances of living our lives in harmony with the Holy Spirit and under an open heaven.

We will grow in proficiency as we learn how to work in symphony with the Holy Spirit and the angels of Christ's Kingdom.

These things will become a normal part of our lives. We will not always need to have an intense spiritual experience or see angels to understand that we can co-labor with them, or to activate or loose God's angels to help us release Christ's Kingdom in our lives. You don't need to see God's angels to work proficiently with them. Many of God's friends will be empowered to walk in this kind of supernatural lifestyle, and working with angels will be considered a normal part of our relationship with Jesus. Angelic ministry will no longer be considered "hyper-spiritual" occurrences. In fact, working with Christ's angels will become commonplace in the near future. I pray that this book will help folks to understand a few dynamics of this approaching release of angelic ministry upon the earth.

As we learn to rend the heavens over our lives, we will begin to understand our true calling. The Holy Spirit will begin to expand our spheres of influence and anointing to proclaim Jesus as the Messiah. Once the heavens are open over us, we will begin to garner the wisdom and revelations of God. We will be born from above and recognize and understand heavenly things. The literal translation of the familiar phrase "born again" is literally "to be born from above" (see John 3:3,16). The Lord will open the heavens over our lives through the outworking of the Holy Spirit as the Spirit reveals, uncovers, or unveils the mysteries of Christ's Kingdom that indwells to us within. Then we will be transformed and actually born from above. We will grow in the power and anointing of the Holy Spirit and into the very image of Jesus. We will begin to recognize and discern heavenly things and see into the spiritual realm on a regular basis. We will develop a heavenly perspective. As a result of living this kind of an "open heaven lifestyle," we can recognize and easily implement Christ's Kingdom in our everyday activities. Supernatural manifestations of God's Kingdom like creative miracles, healings, visions, trances, salvations, and angelic encounters will become a comfortable lifestyle for God's people.

There will be times when God will open our understanding and the eyes of our hearts, allowing us to see and recognize His angelic hosts. God's angels are all around us at this moment. The angels of God are our co-laborers who have the testimony of Jesus, and they are ready to work with us. There is no need to hyper-spiritualize angelic ministry, angelic sightings, or angelic visitations. These should all be a normal part of walking with the Messiah once the heavens are open over our lives.

There are many ways that you can work with God's angels. This should just be a normal part of your daily life as a brother or sister of Jesus or *in* Jesus. Prayer is perhaps the most important and practical way to co-labor with God's angels. I believe that every believer in Messiah has at least one angel that has been assigned to his or her life and ministry. The more obedient and active we become to step out and share our faith in Jesus Christ or go with the Gospel, the more God will accelerate the ministry of His angels within our lives and spheres of influence. As you proclaim, speak, or decree God's truth and His written Word over your life and your family, you will be empowering angels to work on your behalf. God's angels always perform His word (see Ps. 103:20). As we decree God's Word, we activate or loose angels to co-labor with us and to work on our behalf. This scriptural principle makes it very easy for anyone to co-labor with God's angels even if they never actually see one of God's angels!

God's people have the privilege and authority to work with God's angels in many ways. God can release or activate His angels to bring us revelation, protection, provision, and direction. God's angels can bring us messages and release prophecy and prophetic ministry in our midst. The Lord will begin to increase the numbers of people who will consciously work with His angels in releasing the gifts of healings and miracles in these last days as well as many other ways. Many friends of God will become quite proficient and comfortable and will work with Christ's angels to work miracles and healing to people in their sphere of influence. God can release angels at any time or place that the anointing of the Holy Spirit is hovering and in manifestation.

Working with angels will become very common for people as they learn to work in harmony with the Holy Spirit. We can accomplish this through the marvelous unction of the Holy Spirit. The Lord is giving His people a supernatural understanding of the anointing or unction of the Holy Spirit. God is helping them learn how to work in concert or symphony with His Spirit and His Kingdom to glorify Christ as the Messiah.

As we truly begin to understand the anointing and function of the unction of the Holy Spirit, we will begin to implement Jesus' model of prayer upon the earth. We will pray like Christ, and at times the Lord will give folks the authority to loose His angels to accomplish specific assignments or missions of mercy for His glory and honor (see Matt. 16:19; 18:18). Working with angels in this fashion will not always be a "super-spiritual" affair. Rather, at times it will be quite commonplace, and anyone will be able to step into this aspect of the Lord's Kingdom and co-labor with God's angels. This God-ordained ability or gift will come as we grow and begin to understand how the precious Holy Spirit works in symphony with angelic ministry and open heavens to impact the earth for Christ's purpose as it is in Heaven. This dynamic or aspect of Christ's Kingdom is based upon and activated by the restoration of the gift of the discerning of spirits.

Ordinary people will begin to understand and work in harmony with the Holy Spirit. They will have God-ordained revelation of the role of the Holy Spirit in the expanding of their sphere of influence. The key to growing and maturing in this aspect of Christ's Kingdom is repentance and obedience to the Lord's callings and wooing.

What a time to be alive! You are living at the most exciting moment in history. Christ will return soon. The Lord in His wisdom, mercy, and grace is going to use regular folks to implement the greatest revivals and outpourings of His Spirit that have ever touched the earth in the coming days. God is inviting you to take part in releasing these revivals, and He has equipped you to do it. We can rend the heavens over our lives through the finished work of Calvary. We can ascend through the open heavens just like our Messiah, Jesus. We can begin to manifest God's glory and Kingdom in every place that we set our foot.

We have an open invitation to set our feet into the heavenly realms and have communion with Christ. We can ascend into Heaven today and come boldly before our Father. The promise of Hebrews 4:16—*"Let us therefore come boldly to the throne of grace, that we may obtain mercy and find grace to help in time of need"*—is much more than flowery alliteration. This verse is a spiritual truth! We can ascend into the heavens today! The hour of Hebrews 4:16 is at hand! What will it look like in your life when you begin to ascend into and through the open heavens and to enter into the heavenly places?

LOOKING AHEAD

In the next book of this trilogy, I will share dozens of other visions and heavenly experiences with Christ and His angels that transpired in heavenly places. As a result, I can relate to you detailed portraits and descriptions of the places that I walked through in Heaven or the heavenly realms. This will help you to understand in more detail your personal role as a royal priest after the order of Melchizedek. These kinds of open heaven or heavenly experiences do not have to be hyper-spiritual events. Rather, these kinds of supernatural experiences should be normal, and it should be a commonplace event for you to access or ascend through the open heavens and into the very presence of God. Anyone can have this kind of supernatural lifestyle.

The angelic experiences that are outlined in the next book occurred in the spiritual realm, but that does not invalidate their importance or impact upon my life. These testimonies will inspire and encourage you. In fact, several people who have read excerpts from the third book were moved to tears of hope and joy. Heaven is a real place, and the next book of this trilogy describes Heaven's attributes and appearance. I will describe these places in great detail and hopefully give you glimpses into the realms of Heaven. Along this journey, we will also see how angels move about, appear, and seem to work the heavenly realms. This will help you to understand more facets and dynamics of how to co-labor with God's angels. May we all greet one another in that place one day. Heaven is real! And Christ has already prepared a place for you to dwell with Him in Heaven. Your heavenly home awaits you.

I want to encourage you that the testimonies in the subsequent book will bring a smile to your face and joy into your heart as you read them. We hope that you enjoy them and that you find these diminutive portraits of the heart of Jesus and of Heaven beneficial and therapeutic to you today. Ephesians shows us this aspect of the possibilities of our lives in Christ:

God, who is rich in mercy, because of His great love with which He loved us, even when we were dead in trespasses, made us alive together with Christ (by grace you have been saved), and raised us up together, and made us sit together in the heavenly places in Christ Jesus, that in the ages to come He might show the exceeding riches of His grace in His kindness toward us in Christ Jesus. For by grace you have been saved through faith, and that not of yourselves; it is the gift of God (Ephesians 2:4-8).

May the Lord bless you as we journey together into the supernatural realms of Heaven in *Dancing With Angels 3: Angels in the Realms of Heaven.*

OUR ACCESS

Paul the apostle was taken up or caught up into the realms of Heaven and also saw paradise. There is quite a bit of biblical evidence for these kinds of heavenly encounters or experiences. There are numerous examples of this throughout the Bible. Therefore, these kinds of experiences are thoroughly biblical (see 2 Cor. 12:1-3; Ezek. 1:1; Rev. 4:1; Gen. 28:12; 32:2).

Jesus told us:

I go to prepare a place for you. And if I go and prepare a place for you, I will come again and receive you to Myself; that where I am, there you may be also (John 14:2-3).

The Lord is referring to a season of time after His resurrection. That is the hour that we live in now. It is only through the finished work of Christ and the atonement of Calvary that we can hope to access Heaven. It is only through the shed blood of

Christ, which covers humankind's sins, that we can ascend into the heavenly places through God's open heavens. Jesus said: *"I am the way, and the truth, and the life. No one comes to the Father except through Me"* (John 14:6). Jesus Christ is the open heaven. The Lord has sent the Holy Spirit to guide us and to lead us into His very presence and into the heavenly places.

This is a very important key to accessing these kinds of heavenly experiences and angelic visitations. We must come to the Father and to the Father's house or heavenly places through Christ. A person can access the realms of Heaven while he or she lives upon the earth or in this temporal realm though spiritual experiences. Anyone can do this. Hopefully you will also access Heaven when you die and live in Heaven as an eternal spirit. However, as we learned, you can access the realms of Heaven now as a royal priest after the order of Melchizedek.

SALVATION

Perhaps you would like to be born again and receive Jesus as your Lord and Savior now. Just pray this prayer out loud:

Father God, I believe that Jesus Christ is the Savior or Messiah. I believe that Jesus is the only begotten Son of God and that He died upon the Cross to make payment for my sins. I believe that Jesus was buried in an unused grave, but that after three days He rose again to conquer death and sin. Lord, because I was born a human being, I was born a sinner. Lord, I ask You to forgive my sins now in the name of Jesus Christ of Nazareth. God, cover my sins with the blood of Jesus; forgive me now. Amen.

About Kevin Basconi

Kevin and Kathy would love to hear your testimonies about angelic encounters for possible use in future publications. To submit a testimony contact them by e-mail.

King of Glory Ministries International is available to teach the material covered in this book in much greater depth in our *'School of the Supernatural—Dancing With Angels'*.

This school is coming soon in DVD and CD sets.

For more information visit our web page at:
www.kingofgloryministries.org.

Email King of Glory Ministries International at:
info@kingofgloryministries.org.

Call King of Glory Ministries International at:
336-921-2825 or 816-225-8224

or send us your mail at:
King of Glory Ministries International
P. O. Box 903, Moravian Falls, NC 28654

Please visit our online art gallery to help support our humanitarian outreaches to help build homes for at risk children and feed widows and orphans at:
www.MoravianFallsminiatureartgallery.com

A portion of all sales of art purchased from this site will be used to help feed orphans in Third World nations. Thanks for your support in this worthwhile cause.

You can also donate directly to our humanitarian works in the Third World. If you are a citizen of Canada, America, or the UK you can give directly through Hope For The Nations and your gift will be tax deductible in your home nation.

Look for the Hope For The Nations link on the King of Glory Ministries web page, or surf to www.hopeforthenations.com.

Kevin and Kathy will be donating 90% of net proceeds from this book to those individuals and ministries who are building orphanages, helping widows and orphans, and preaching the Gospel to the poor and lost of the earth.

Thanks for your help with this by your purchase of this book.

Other Books by Kevin Basconi

Dancing With Angels 1:
How You Can Work With Angels in Your Life

IN THE RIGHT HANDS, THIS BOOK WILL CHANGE LIVES!

Most of the people who need this message will not be looking for this book. To change their lives, you need to put a copy of this book in their hands.

> *But others (seeds) fell into good ground, and brought forth fruit, some a hundred-fold, some sixty-fold, some thirty-fold* (Matthew 13:8).

Our ministry is constantly seeking methods to find the good ground, the people who need this anointed message to change their lives. Will you help us reach these people?

> *Remember this—a farmer who plants only a few seeds will get a small crop. But the one who plants generously will get a generous crop* (2 Corinthians 9:6).

EXTEND THIS MINISTRY BY SOWING
3 BOOKS, 5 BOOKS, 10 BOOKS, OR MORE TODAY,
AND BECOME A LIFE CHANGER!

Thank you,

Don Nori Sr., Founder
Destiny Image
Since 1982

DESTINY IMAGE PUBLISHERS, INC.

*"Speaking to the Purposes of God for This Generation
and for the Generations to Come."*

VISIT OUR NEW SITE HOME AT
WWW.DESTINYIMAGE.COM

FREE SUBSCRIPTION TO DI NEWSLETTER

Receive free unpublished articles by top DI authors, exclusive

discounts, and free downloads from our best and newest books.

Visit www.destinyimage.com to subscribe.

Write to: Destiny Image
              P.O. Box 310
              Shippensburg, PA 17257-0310

Call: 1-800-722-6774

Email: orders@destinyimage.com

For a complete list of our titles or to place an order
online, visit www.destinyimage.com.

FIND US ON FACEBOOK OR FOLLOW US ON TWITTER.

www.facebook.com/destinyimage   facebook
www.twitter.com/destinyimage   twitter